My Memories of
JIM REEVES
...and other celebrities
by Joyce Gray Jackson

N☀VA
B O O K S

For a complete list of Nova Books Nashville titles,
check out: *www.novabooksnashville.com*

"My Memories of Jim Reeves
. . . And Other Celebrities"

(c) 2009 by Nova Books Nashville
All Rights Reserved

Catalog data:

Jackson, Joyce Gray
With Forewords by Jeannie Seely & Kitty Wells

Original ISBN # 0-9632684-7-3 (hdc : alk. paper)

Original ISBN # 0-9632684-6-5 (pbk : alk. paper)

Original ISBN # 0-9632684-8-1 (e-bk.)

p. cm series (American Arts Culture)

ACKNOWLEDGEMENTS

We are grateful to the following for their varied contributions to the publishing of this work, authored by Joyce Gray Jackson, and published by Nova Books Nashville, in affiliation with Lightning Source, Inc., LaVergne, TN: Cover executed by Tom Barkoukis, Barkoukis Design, Nashville; text input by Arnold Rogers, Carmel Enterprises, Nashville; editing by Bill Brough and Ruth White, and additional production and photo scanning by Nova Books Nashville staff. Thanks also to the Country Music Hall of Fame & Library; RCA Records; Billboard Publications, Inc.; SOURCE Nashville Foundation; and to the former Jim Reeves Enterprises. Photos not supplied by the author, are from the collections of Patricia Presley, Marsha Basore and Walt Trott.

The Grand Ladies

JEANNIE SEELY, a free spirit, was the first star to wear mini-skirts on the historic, but staid *Grand Ole Opry* program. This gifted vocalist from Pennsylvania, won a Grammy award for her very first *Billboard* chart record, "Don't Touch Me," in 1966, a song written by her husband-to-be Hank Cochran. She is also a writer of note, having contributed a Top 10 song to her late friend Faron Young in 1971, "Leavin' and Sayin' Goodbye," to others such as Connie Smith, Ray Price and Dottie West, and she authored "Pieces Of a Puzzled Mind," a book of amusing anecdotes penned in 1989. Since 1967, she's been a regular cast member  of WSM's legendary *Grand Ole Opry,* and her numerous hits have included such standards as "I'll Love You More," "Wish I Didn't Have To Miss You" (with Jack Greene), "Lucky Ladies" and "Can I Sleep in Your Arms (Tonight, Mister)."

KITTY WELLS, hailed as the Queen of Country Music, is a Nashville native who has recorded in several decades. She earned a #1 Gold Record with her first *Billboard* charting "It Wasn't God Who Made Honky Tonk Angels," the first ever for a country female. No one-hit wonder, she amassed over 40 Top 10 singles and albums, before being voted into the Country Music Hall of Fame in 1976. Among the legends she has sung with were Hank Williams, Roy Acuff, Red Foley and Webb Pierce, while her opening acts have  included such legends-to-be as Elvis Presley and Patsy Cline. In 1991, Kitty received a Lifetime Grammy Award for her many career achievements, citing such additional #1s as "One By One" and "Heartbreak USA." Upcoming is her Nova Books biography, "Kitty Wells, Makin' Believe."

FOREWORDS

Having been fortunate enough to be a part of the same era in Nashville as Joyce Jackson, I was delighted when I heard she was writing a book about it. Sharing her memories has brought back so many of my own! It is refreshing to hear the candid stories from that time period, told by someone who was really there. Joyce was a living part of the day-to-day workings on Music Row, while I was traveling on the road, so it is fascinating how events often coincided. Unfortunately, I did not have the opportunity to meet Jim Reeves personally, but I have always admired him as an artist and as a businessman, so I especially appreciate Joyce giving us such a rare glimpse into his private life. This book is a great contribution to the history of country music.

Jeannie Seely

WSM's *Grand Ole Opry*

I met Joyce in Louisville, Ky., in 1957, while doing a show there. However, our friendship actually began in 1962, through her working at Jim Reeves Enterprises. Through the years, Joyce has become a dear and close friend to me and my family. Joyce has been a dedicated and loyal fan to the music business, as well as playing an important role in the working part of the industry. I am proud to be a part of Joyce's book and I know you will enjoy reading her unique stories. Sincerely . . .

Kitty Wells

Country Music Hall of Fame

AUTHOR'S DEDICATION

There is not enough room on this page to dedicate this book to everyone that I would like to, but you know I love you anyway.

To my Mom and Dad, Wiley and Sue Gray, for not only giving me life, but the freedom and encouragement to try my many endeavors. They are in their home on high now, but God, how I loved you both.

To my daughter Joy, who has been a joy to me in every sense of the word and for her "go for it Mom" attitude in whatever I tried to do, and to Dennis, Joy's husband, for loving her and their three boys: Wiley, Jacob and Colton-Lee.

To my sisters, Glenda, Jan and Marsha, who have stood by me even though they didn't always know where I was coming from, and to Ruby Taylor (Johnnie Wright and Kitty Wells' daughter), who also stood by me through whatever (until her death on Sept. 27, 2009)! To my brother Jerry and his wife Shirley (Shirley passed away in May 1998), and to Jerry B., Bob and Stu, my brothers -in-law, who have always been more like brothers.

To my best friend Perla Harkins for being a best friend in every way and her husband, Dan, whom I would like to clone for me. To my faith sister, Werdna Moss and to Coleen Ruperto, Barbara Byrd and Yvette Owen (now deceased), who need no explanation. To my spiritual kids, Don and Kim, who have always been in my corner and to Yohanna, my daughter from Honduras (she was an exchange student when she and Joy were freshmen and I love her as if she were my daughter). To Mae Axton, my other "Mama," need I say more? Thanks Mae. (Mae died in 1997.)

To my Montana friends, Bill and Melissa Rains, Charlean Keller (Charlean passed on in 2004) and to Denny and P.J. Eubanks (yes, I used the tape recorder!).

To Aunt Iva (Mom's sister, who is now with Mom & Dad) and to Uncle Bob.

To Ralph Emery, my Danish friends Mogens and Hanne, Jim's niece Lani, Larry Jordan, and the many Jim Reeves' fans from all over the world. Thank you. To Aaron at Wal-Mart, just because!

To my special friend Katherine Sutcliffe, a *New York Times'* best-selling author of historical romances, who said she'd pull this book out of me. Thanks Kathy, you'll never know just how much knowing you has helped me.

⊰ IN MEMORY ⊱

Leo Jackson, lead guitar player for the late Jim Reeves, my dear friend of over 50 years, my ex-husband and my daughter Joy's dad, passed away May 4, 2008. He was a very talented guitar player and will be missed by the music industry and by his family and friends.

After the death of Jim Reeves, Leo remained as a member of the Blue Boys with Bud Logan heading the group as their lead singer, and worked many sessions playing on all of the early Alabama recordings.

Leo has traveled all over the world and played an important role in the one and only Jim Reeves' movie, "Kimberley Jim," filmed in South Africa. He became friends with Arne Benoni, an artist from Norway, who looked up to and loved Jim's music. Leo traveled to Norway many times to tour with Arne. He also played on Arne's sessions that were done in Nashville, producing some of these sessions, as well.

Leo and I shared many wonderful years of friendship and had a special bond that we agreed that nothing or no one would ever be able to break. I loved him dearly and he did me, as well as being friends and shared many topics that friends do. There are those who would disagree with me on this matter, but then they aren't the ones that shared the talks, the years and the love that we did.

I miss you Leo, and still find it hard to believe that you are truly gone. I look forward to seeing you again after my time is up here in this world. I hope and pray that you are now at peace.

Joyce Gray Jackson

AUTHOR'S INTRODUCTION

I moved to Nashville, Jan. 19, 1958. Ten days later, I was working for *Gentleman Jim Reeves*. I was with Jim until his untimely death six-and-a-half years later (July 31, 1964). I remained with Jim Reeves Enterprises until Jan. 31, 1988. I lived and worked in Nashville for close to 50 years, and while there I had the opportunity to meet and become friends with many people in the music industry. Some I got to know better than others. I now live near Colorado Springs, Colo., but still stay in touch with my family and friends in Nashville.

There will be many mentions of the RCA Building and of Linebaugh's Restaurant, as well as mentioning some of the same ones in the different stories, but this has to be, as much of my past life and how it crossed those that I've written about, took place at these establishments and with each other. These same people also crossed the lives of many of you. Their lives are worth sharing and even repeating. I just had to write this book, so that my memories of these wonderful people could be documented. This is not going to be a "tell all" book, even though I could tell a lot! I personally feel enough has been written along those lines. It is simply a book showing how my life's path crossed the paths of people on the music scene and other related entertainment industries.

On July 30, 2009, the SOURCE Foundation in Nashville honored me for the work that I have done in the past to help promote country music. The foundation was established to uplift the women who have played a vital part in the industry, but seldom get to enjoy any recognition for their work. It was established in 1991, but this was the seventh year that they have had an awards banquet and presented plaques to those they're honoring. I was pleased to be the recipient of such a classy award. It was indeed an honor and I am truly thankful. This is one more memory that I am most happy to share.

Until now, these have been just *my memories,* but I feel they are good memories and worth sharing. I hope you will feel the same way I do, because with the help of God, it is a pleasure to be sharing "My Memories Of Jim Reeves . . . And Other Celebrities."

PREFACE

Mary Reeves was truly the keeper of the flame. Following the tragic death of her 40-year-old singer-songwriter husband Jim Reeves in a plane crash near Nashville in 1964, she worked in liaison with his label, RCA Records.

They wisely chose to ration out his unreleased records as singles over the next two decades, stretching his already booming international career. As a result, his albums still sell in this, the 21st century, both here and abroad, .

Mary White met Jim Reeves in 1946, after he had been pitching for the St. Louis Cardinals farm team for three years. After slipping on a wet mound, he nearly severed the sciatic nerve in his left leg, which ended his hopes for a major league career. He and Mary were wed in 1947.

Turning to his second love, the Texan from Panola County, started working with the radio station that owned the ball team. As his radio audience increased, Jim began singing in clubs. It wasn't until music mogul Fabor Robinson caught his act, however, that he recorded, naturally enough for Fabor's independent label, Abbott Records in 1952.

Backed by the Circle O Ranch Boys band, Reeves scored a #1 record on "Mexican Joe," an upbeat ballad written by Mitchell Torok, another Abbott artist (who himself hit #1 with his self-penned "Caribbean" that same year). "Mexican Joe" hit the top of *Billboard's* country chart May 9, 1953, and stayed perched up there nine weeks.

By then, Jim was working on KWKH-Shreveport's *Louisiana Hayride,* and also hosted his own nightly *Red River Round-Up* program weekdays as a DJ at the station. Reeves' very next release, the uptempo novelty tune "Bimbo," also hit #1, Jan. 9, 1954, holding in that position three weeks, another home run for the ex-ballplayer. He followed those introductory number ones with a trio of Top 10s: "I Love You" (with Ginny Wright), "Penny Candy" and "Drinking Tequila," the latter in the spring of 1955.

After ending his association with Abbott that year, Reeves signed with the major label RCA, home to legends like the late Jimmie Rodgers, Eddy Arnold, Hank Snow and later Elvis Presley. His first hit for RCA was his own composition "Yonder Comes a Sucker," a Top Five in late '55.

After a trio of Top 10s - "My Lips Are Sealed," "According To My Heart" and "Am I Losing You" (which would become a hit all over again three years later in 1960) - Jim again hit #1 with the classic "Four Walls," May 27, 1957, for eight weeks, and it also became his first pop hit peaking at #11. Following five more Top 10 singles, he again scored a five-week chart-topper with "Billy Bayou," written by Roger Miller, on *Billboard's* Jan. 19, 1959 list. Top Fives followed: "Home," again by Miller, and "Partners" by Danny Dill.

Then came his biggest hit ever, "He'll Have To Go," which was #1 for 14 weeks during its 34-week *Billboard* charting period, and it became Reeves' first million-seller. It crossed over into the pop charts, scoring #2 in 1960, also #13 on the R&B chart, and has since become a Grammy Hall of Fame Record.

In 1964, Jim did a duet with his friend Dottie West on the Justin Tubb song "Love Is

No Excuse," yet another Top 10. Jim Reeves has attained 51 Top 10 records, including such classics as "Anna Marie," "Blue Boy," "I Missed Me," "Adios Amigo," "Welcome To My World," "Snow Flake," "When Two Worlds Collide" and "Missing You."

A month after his death, Reeves' "I Guess I'm Crazy" hit the coveted #1 spot, marking six chart-toppers on the artist, whose career seemed suddenly cut short. But under the loving guidance and marketing *know how* of his widow, he would garner another five #1 records: "This Is It," "Is It Really Over?," "Distant Drums," "Blue Side of Lonesome" and "I Won't Come In While He's There."

Albums released from 1964-1983 include four #1 LPs: "Moonlight & Roses," "The Best of Jim Reeves," "Up Through the Years" and "Distant Drums." Other near-chart-topping sets include "The Jim Reeves Way," "Yours Sincerely, Jim Reeves," "Blue Side of Lonesome" and "A Touch of Sadness." From 1964 onward, RCA sold a total 13 Top 10 Jim Reeves' albums.

Oddly enough, thanks to engineering wizardry, there's a 1981 "Greatest Hits: Jim Reeves & Patsy Cline" Top 10 album, featuring the two deceased artists (who never sang together in their lifetimes), dueting on selections such as the old Ernest Tubb classic "Have You Ever Been Lonely," which spun off as a hit single for them, peaking Top Five on Jan. 30, 1982.

Incidentally, Mary helped arrange for newcomer Deborah Allen to "duet" with Jim in 1979, resulting in three Top 10 singles, all through the wonders of electronics: "Don't Let Me Cross Over," "Oh, How I Miss You Tonight" and "Take Me In Your Arms and Hold Me." (She was 10 years old when Jim died.)

Jim Reeves, who became an Opry member in 1955, was inducted posthumously into the Country Music Hall of Fame in 1967.

Jim Reeves off stage.

Jim does some publicty shots a la 'Adios Amigo.'

Joyce's Who's Who...

Joyce's Who's Who...

Jim spoofs Thomas Gainsborough's classic 1770 painting 'Blue Boy' ... the title of which proved a major song hit for Reeves in 1958, as composed by Boudleaux Bryant.

Meet JIM REEVES...

Jan. 28, 1958 is a date that changed my life. That was the day that *Gentleman Jim Reeves* hired me to become his secretary. How do I begin to write about this wonderful singer, gentle man and friend? There is so much to tell and I had put off writing about Jim, because it's hard even today for me to talk or write about both Jim and Mary, without shedding a few tears. Much has been written and said about Jim over the past years since his early death in that terrible plane crash, July 31, 1964, and I know that I will be critiqued by many, but this is my story and my memory, and I must tell it in my own way.

I don't mean to sound harsh, but frankly I am so tired of everyone thinking they knew so much about Jim, when what most of them know is what they've heard from others or what someone else has written. They just didn't know the man! I did. You don't work as closely with someone as Jim and I did, with our desks cornered and not get to know the person as well as the singer, so I will start my story from the beginning.

I came to Nashville on Jan. 19, 1958, with two suitcases and $150. I told my Mom that if I didn't have a job in two weeks that I would come home. I was 21 years old, almost 22, and she assured me that she would be there if I needed her.

I spent a great deal of my first few days down at a 24-hour meat-and-three restaurant called Linebaugh's that was located a couple of doors from the Ernest Tubb Record Shop and just around the corner from the Ryman Auditorium, which housed the *Grand Ole Opry* at that time.

It was during one of these visits when Bob Holt (Bob was promotion man for RCA at that time) came in, and since I was sitting alone asked if he might join me. I told him that he could, as there were no strangers in Linebaugh's, although I had never met Bob before then.

In the course of our conversation, he asked what I was doing in Nashville and I told him I was looking for a job. He said he knew someone who was looking for a girl. That someone was Herb Shucher, who was the manager for Jim Reeves. He gave me the office phone number and I called the next day, which was on Jan. 26. Herb was out when I called and Jim answered the phone, but since I didn't know who it was I told him I would call back a little later, and Jim said Herb should be back in about 10 minutes. I did call back and set up an appointment for the next day.

At that time, Jim was doing his daily ABN Radio series from Studio C in the old National Life Building where WSM originated. Herb and I had a good discussion about the job and he asked if I would be willing to go up to Studio C and talk with Jim. Of course, I said I would and he called to let Jim know that I would be coming up to meet with him after his show. I got there and saw the last 30 minutes of *The Jim Reeves Show.* It was the only one I got to see. We met in the artists' lounge which was actually just a foyer for the men's restroom, and I believe there were mail slots for the various artists who were members of the Opry. We discussed the job at great length and Jim asked if I could come to the office the next day and talk with him and Herb together. I said yes, and I got to the office in Primrose Center around 9 a.m. on the 28th.

Jim had me sit in his office across the room from his desk. So many people came into the office that day beginning with Mary, Jim's wife, and Charlie Rhoten. Charlie was in real estate and had a contract to build Jim and Mary's new home. Leo Jackson also came in. He was home on leave from the Army. Jim Ed, Maxine and Bonnie Brown all came by. The Browns were in town to record and at that time they lived in Arkansas. Jim introduced me to everyone that came in and I had no idea that I was being scrutinized for the job, but I suppose I was. A little after noon, Jim finally told Herb to come into his office, so we could all discuss the job. Herb came in and pulled up a chair beside Jim and here I sat across the room with both of them looking at me, this little young girl from Kentucky, who didn't know anything about the music business except that I liked it. I'll admit that I was more than a little nervous, but then Jim turned to Herb and said, "When do you want her to go to work?" Herb said, "In the morning." That's all there was to it. I started working for Jim the next day. I called Mom and told her I would not be coming back home, because I had just been hired by Jim Reeves as his secretary. She was very excited and needless to say, so was I.

One of the first people I met after I started working for Jim was Sam Wallace, who was the RCA promotion man from Atlanta. He was in town and had come to what was then called the *Friday Night Frolics* (later to be called the *Friday Night Opry*). I had gone to the show because Jim was on and I wanted to see him perform. He introduced me to Sam as his new secretary and asked me to join him and Sam for a bite to eat. We went to the Hickory Room at the old Andrew Jackson Hotel.

Sam passed away several years ago, but was one of the nicest men I ever met. I remember one time that some friends of mine and I went to Atlanta and I called Sam and told him I was coming down, and he took us all to dinner. It was a catfish place where you could eat all you wanted. We had such a good time. Sam did so much to promote Jim and his music over the southeastern U.S.

I wish I could remember all the different ones that I met that night at the *Friday Night Frolics,* but I can't. I know Faron Young was there, though I had met Faron a year before, when I had come to Nashville to visit. That's another story in this book.

Some of the first things I had to do as Jim's secretary was to write to disc jockeys (D.J.'s) all over the country and thank them for playing his latest record, "Anna Marie," written by Cindy Walker, and I also acquired the title President of the Jim Reeves Fan Club and had to contact all the many members. That's how I first met Doris Gath, who lived in Minnesota and was vice-president of the fan club. She and Elmer had become personal friends of Jim's and I believe they came down for a visit later that same year and that's when I met them. We've been friends all these years. They have even visited me in Colorado.

I was living on the west end of Nashville and had to ride a bus into town, and then transfer to another bus that was going out to Madison, where Jim's office was. That was no problem, as the bus stopped close to the office, but when Jim and Herb dissolved their business relationship in October 1959, I was still riding and transferring buses, and since we had moved the office to the house that meant someone would have to pick me up at the bus stop. Sometimes Mary would do this and a lot of times Jim would be there to pick me up. Many times, however, I spent the night at the house, especially if Jim had to do a night session. He would ask me to stay, so he could play the session for Mary and me when he came home. We'd wait up and listen to the session. That was always special to me because it made me feel as though I was really a part of Jim's music career. They had a guest room that was designated as mine whenever I stayed. Leo Jackson (Jim's guitarist) also had a room. He not only had a room, but lived with them for a period of time before Jim formed his Blue Boys band. Jim and Mary treated Leo and me like we were their kids. They had no children, so guess we were substitutes. That was OK with me, as I feel it was for Leo.

Because I worked for Jim, I was afforded the opportunity to meet many people in the music and other related businesses, and my life has been made richer because of Jim, Mary and all these wonderful people. Jim was a great person to work for; however, since he was such a perfectionist, it was at times a bit difficult, but the band and I realized that Jim just wanted things done his way, which we did.

It wasn't all work being Jim's secretary. There were parties for Jim's and Mary's birthdays and at Christmas time, and there were times that Jim would come to the office and just sit there with his guitar and sing some crazy little ditty. I remember asking him where he'd found such a song and he said his mother taught it to him when he was a little boy. This happened quite often, especially when we moved to Jim's house and fixed up one end of the basement for our offices. When we first moved to the house, our office was put in their den and we stayed there until 1962, then moved to the basement. While we were in the den, I got a phone call on their home phone - as Jim was talking to Harlan Howard on the office phone - saying that my Dad had been accidentally shot. It was in March 1961, and I had to get to him as chances of survival were slim. I heard Jim tell Harlan he had to hang up that something was seriously wrong. I told him what had happened and that I must get to him. He got on the phone and called American Airlines and demanded they get me a seat which they did and then told Dean Manuel, his pianist and road manager, to take me to the airport. Dean started driving me and as we neared the end of Jim's road, there sat a Sheriff's patrol car.

Dean asked if he would escort us to the airport, after explaining our situation. The officer said he was not allowed to do that, but he would take me himself! He did and I made it to the airport ahead of time and was even able to catch an earlier flight. My Dad did not survive and died two days after my 25th birthday. Even on his death bed, he teased me about being his old maid daughter! What a wonderful Dad I had. He loved Jim's music and was so proud that I was his secretary. Dad was a truck driver and when he'd stop at truck stops, he'd play Jim's records on the jukeboxes across the country. Then he'd tell some of them that his daughter worked for Jim and, of course, they never believed him.

Never again did we see a patrol car at that spot. Call it what you want to, but I feel God had sent an Angel to help me. This was just one of the many wonderful things that Jim did for others. I recall there was a lady in San Antonio, Texas, who was a big fan of Jim's and she was quite elderly. I don't remember who informed Jim that her record player didn't work anymore and she was saddened because she could no longer play his records. So he called the Perry Shankle Company in San Antonio, and told them to send a record player to her and send him the bill.

Another time someone in North Carolina sent us a newspaper clipping about this little blind girl who was a big fan of Jim's. She was only 9 or 10 years of age and wanted either a Braille Bible or a Braille watch. Jim told me to find her a Braille Bible. It just so happened that my first job after graduating from high school was printing Braille books, and I knew this would not be possible. I explained this to Jim, so we got a Braille watch and sent it to her. We got the sweetest letter from the little girl's mother. Jim was a kind, wonderful man and not what some tend to say about him. He was a businessman and since music was his business, he treated it as such and there were some who did not like the way he handled his business, but I feel that was their problem.

Also while we had our offices in the den, Jim was asked to be on *The Jimmy Dean Show* that originated from New York. Jim's hair was beginning to gray a little around the temples and he would often get it dyed. Two days before he was to leave for New York, he decided to color it himself. I've told this story in interviews before and I know it will be in author Larry Jordan's forthcoming book on Jim, but I just have to tell it here in mine and perhaps a new fan or reader will enjoy it, if they have never heard it before. At any rate, Jim did try to color his hair and evidently used too much developer and instead of it dying his hair the color he wanted, it turned out orange! I mean orange like carrot orange. Like I said before, after we moved to our offices to the house, Mary or Jim would pick me up at the bus stop. Well this morning, Mary picked me up and told me what Jim had done and asked me not to laugh at him when I saw him. That was the wrong thing to ask of me! I was sitting at Jim's desk, going through the mail that Mary and I had gotten from the post office, when I heard Jim come down the hall. I would not look up, as I knew what to expect and just kept my head down, looking at the mail. When he asked if there was anything important in it, I said no, just the usual.

He then proceeded to tell me what he had done and, of course, I had to look up and when I did, I couldn't help myself, I burst out laughing and could not stop. I guess you had to be there, but this was one of the funniest sights that I had ever seen. The laughter was catching and soon Jim was laughing, instead of getting mad and said, "What am I going to do, so that I can get to New York and to a salon and have this color done right?" I suggested that he get some Nestle's Hair Color Rinse and temporarily color it. He then sent me out to get the rinse. Long story short, he did his hair, got to New York and did the show.

Jim was one of the funniest people that I ever knew. He once told me that if he was as funny to everyone as he was to me, that he would change his profession and be a comedian instead of a singer. He had so many funny sayings. He told Clarence Selman one time that if he ever fell out of a chair, it would take him five minutes to hit the floor! He also told Clarence that he was "as slow as cream rising on a stump," whoever heard the like! Guess you had to be raised on a farm to know that cream rises to the top and, of course, not on a stump, which made Clarence extremely slow! He was by the way. Clarence has now passed away.

I was able to see Jim perform on the *Grand Ole Opry* many times, but only got to see one of his performances on the road. It was in East Point, Ga., at an old school that had been converted into a theater. I have mentioned this theater in other places in the book. I was dating James Kirkland at the time and James was then the lead singer of the Blue Boys band and fronted (performing before Jim came on) Jim's show. James and the other Blue Boys - Leo Jackson, Mel Rogers and Dean Manuel - did this comedy act called The Lump, Lump Boys, Art, Mart, Bart and Fargo. They were extremely funny and I wanted to catch their act, so one of my roommates, Angie Phariss and Bob Bradley (she later married Bob) and I drove to East Point and caught the show. We enjoyed the Blue Boys portion of the show and the Lump Lumps, and when Jim came on stage he looked down and saw me and asked what I was doing there? I said to finally see one of his shows. He made me stand up and introduced me to the audience. I was a bit embarrassed, but at the same time it made me feel good that he did this. Another time that I was able to see him perform, other than at the Opry, was in Centennial Park in Nashville, where he performed with the Nashville Symphony Orchestra. Mary, Cindy Walker and I sat on the ground in front of the stage to watch him. What a wonderful night and memory that was. I'm not telling this story of my association with Jim in any kind of order, but I feel that is OK and perhaps even makes the story better.

Jim is mentioned throughout this book anyway, as he was such a part of the lives of some of the others that I have written about, including Red Foley. When Red was ill and had to leave his show out in Springfield, Mo., Jim was called on to host the show, called *Jubilee USA*. It was called *Ozark Jubilee* before that. He only did it for a couple of months.

"Cheyenne," Jim and Mary's Collie dog, would sit and watch Jim as he did the show. You could tell he knew that it was Jim. Cheyenne and Jim had a great relationship and there were times that Jim would ask me to go out and play with Cheyenne, because he knew Cheyenne was lonesome. Cheyenne would come to the sliding glass doors when our office was in the den and shake and shiver, even though it would be hot outside, so someone would let him in. Of course, Jim always let him inside. We all loved that dog. I remember one time someone was coming to the house to bring Jim some songs and I forgot that Cheyenne was in the house. I went to the back door to let the man in and Cheyenne would have nailed him if Jim hadn't run to us and grabbed Cheyenne, and held him until the man could give me the tape. He was as protective of me as he was of Mary and Jim, but that was because our office was there in the house, so he knew I belonged. When I remember Cheyenne, it reminds me of the time when Jim and Mary had gone to Texas and I was staying at their house (I did this many times when they would be gone). I had been out mowing their yard and playing with Cheyenne and had pulled the back door to and didn't realize it was in the lock position. I had no way of getting in, so I broke the bottom pane of the back door and let myself in, then called a repairman to come and put the pane back in. Sometime later Jim went outside and locked himself out. We were talking about it one day and I asked him how much it cost him to have the pane put back in and he said it was around four or five dollars and I told him that it had only cost me 77 cents. He gave me a shocked look and asked when I had locked myself out. I told him it was when he and Mary had gone on vacation in Texas. We had a good laugh about it.

Jim was never one to hand out compliments to your face, but he would be proud of you to others. I know Ann Tant told me one time that they were talking to him during one of his trips to Atlanta and when they asked how I was doing he told them that I was fine and if I ever left him he just might as well cut off his right arm. This, of course, made me very happy to hear, as it was a nice compliment. I guess the closest he ever got to complimenting me to my face was during one of the early DJ Conventions. It was either the one in 1958 or 1959. RCA had a hospitality suite in the old Andrew Jackson Hotel on the 11th floor, and I went up to say hello to Pat Kelleher and some others that I had met, and Jim was there talking to George Parkhill. I said hello to him and George wanted to know who I was, and Jim said, "George, I'm proud to say this is my secretary."

Jim was really great to work for and he worked at his craft diligently. When he would be preparing for a session, he'd play and sing along with the selections over and over and live with them, then he would put them up for a little while, then get them out again, and if they felt the same way to him he would take them into the studio to record. When he did those *Afrikaans* albums in South Africa, he would play the songs and learn them phonetically. It was wonderful to have been privileged to watch him work.

Jim was also a big pushover for a sob story. I remember this guy coming to the house dressed as a priest and said he was from Canada, and while traveling had run into some bad luck. His car had broken down and he had run out of money and was more or less looking for a hand out. Jim called Faron Young and told him the story and asked if he would go in with him and help this priest out. Faron agreed to do so and they called the Andrew Jackson Hotel to arrange a room for him. Jim took him to the

Andrew Jackson and they told management to allow him room service. After a couple of days, the manager of the hotel called Jim and told him that the man was ordering whiskey, and he felt that was a bit strange for a priest down-on-his-luck to be doing. Needless to say, Jim and Faron put a stop to it all, but not before he had run up quite a bill! Then there was a woman in Georgia, who wanted Jim to adopt her baby, and Jim wanted to and then he told Mary about it. Mary put her foot down and said, "No way, Jim, think about it. She would know who had the baby and would always be needing money or something from you. It's just not the thing to do." He agreed and this, of course, didn't happen. I'm just showing a side of Jim that most would not know. Some have painted him as not being a nice person and that is just not true, and I want to let the world know the real Jim Reeves, the one that was my boss and my friend.

Jim knew that he was gaining popularity all over the world and this made him extremely happy, and when "He'll Have to Go" reached the million mark, he couldn't believe it. It was a fun time for all of us, watching this song go to #1 in the country charts, as well as #2 Pop and #13 R&B. It charted 31 weeks, 14 of which ranked at #1, and became a Grammy Hall of Fame Recording.

I went to the Opry the night that Chet Atkins presented Jim with the Gold Record. It was April 1960. Jim has now been gone 45 years, which means that I'm that much older and even though my memory is still good, times and dates don't always match the event.

One day while sitting in the office, after he had received the gold record, I asked Jim what it felt like to have attained the ultimate goal that any singer desires to reach? He said that it felt good, but that he knew he had not done it alone and there were many who helped him reach this point; Mary, RCA Records, and all their field men, the Blue Boys, the DJs that had faithfully played his record, and he even gave me credit.

Jim was an avid golfer and a member of the Bluegrass Country Club in nearby Hendersonville, Tenn. He had his own golf cart. It was blue and had a fringed top on it. He was about a 12 handicapper and often played with Chet, Archie Campbell and Porter Wagoner. I'm sure there were others in the business he played with from time-to-time, but those are a few that I remember.

One of my fondest memories was when Jim had played the title role in South African filmmaker Emil Nofal's movie "Kimberley Jim." There was a sneak preview at the Martin Theatre in Clarksville, Tenn. Jim, Mary, Leo, Dean, Ray Baker and I all went to the premiere. Jim sat between Ray and me, so he could explain all about the movie and the different locations where they filmed. I really wanted to watch the movie, but knowing that he was describing the various areas where some of the people lived we had corresponded with, I paid attention to him and missed most of what the film was about.

Of course, I have a copy of the movie now and have watched it many times. Jim would have been a good actor, had he the opportunity to pursue this facet of the entertainment business. Actually, he wanted to do more movies and one was reportedly in the works.

One year, we had a birthday party for Jim that was an outside affair. He liked Black Jack Daniel's whiskey. He didn't drink much, but when he did have a drink, that was his choice. I had given him a bottle for his birthday and he opened it up at the party, saying I had to take the poison out by drinking the first drink from the bottle. I don't like whiskey, but everyone was cheering me on, so I took the poison out!

Mary was an excellent bowler and one time when I picked Jim up at the airport, we stopped back by the Melrose Bowling Lanes where Mary's team was playing and as we were walking up the sidewalk, Jim said, "Joyce, you should sue the city." Why?, I asked. "For pouring this sidewalk so close to your butt!" We had a good laugh because you see I'm only 5-foot tall and, of course, Jim was close to 6-feet. He was always coming up with something that made me laugh!

During the six-and-a-half years that I was Jim's secretary, there was only one time that we kinda locked horns. I don't even remember what it was about, but I know I told Jim that he was wrong about something, and he didn't like it, and told me that if I didn't watch out, I would be looking for another job. That made me mad and I looked him straight in the eye and said that I was looking for a job when I found that one! I began slamming desk drawers shut . . . and he realized I was truly mad and before the day was over, he had me laughing. We neither one ever apologized to the other. It was never brought up again either.

I got a letter one time at my office in the RCA Building and the stamp on it was one bearing Jim's likeness that had been included in the "Something Special" album and it wasn't even a real postage stamp, but the postal department let it go through and even cancelled it. Here is a photo of the envelope with the stamp of Jim on it. I always felt that was rather interesting.

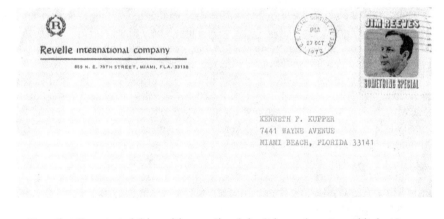

Now that I've started this writing on Jim, I don't know how to end it, but I suppose now would be a good time to talk about the day he left for Batesville, Ark., to look at some property. It's amazing to me how everyone thought that Jim had asked them to go with him. I know he had asked Hank Cochran to go and I believe he had asked Leo or maybe it was Dean that asked Leo to go, and I know that he had asked Ray Baker to go. Hank couldn't make it because of some prior commitment and I don't know why Leo couldn't go, but Ray Baker had a demo session he had to take part in, so he asked Dean to go and, of course, Dean went. You can't believe the people in Nashville that claim that they were supposed to be with him. Jim would have had to rent a big jet plane to take them all! They have even tried to convince me that Jim had called them, but the fact is that just isn't the case. The ones that I have mentioned are the only ones that I know anything about Jim asking them to go. A lot of controversy has taken place regarding the day that Jim left, and it has me wondering where all these people were on this particular day.

I know they weren't at our office. I know where I was and I also know where Jim was, and this is how the events of the day took place. Jim had called Mr. Griffith, the man he was to meet with in Batesville and confirmed their appointment. Ray Baker was about to leave for his session and Jim went out to talk with him, standing by the open car door for about 45 minutes, until I called him into the office, as he had a phone call from Fred Bunyan at Berry Field, the place where Jim had rented the plane. Jim came in, Ray left and he confirmed everything with Fred for later that afternoon. He then went outside and set out some plants that Mary had gotten for Christmas. She had been trying to get him to set them out for quite some time and he picked this morning to do so. He came in with sweat dripping from his forehead and said, "Thank God for air conditioning."

We laughed about it, then the phone rang and it was Mary. She was calling from Old Hickory Golf and Country Club where she had been playing in a golf tournament. She lost and Jim told her that he knew she would lose because earlier that morning while having breakfast she had talked herself out of the win. They planned to meet a little later at Third National Bank, so he could say goodbye and get monies for his trip. He then went upstairs, showered and got ready to go and came back down to the office to let me know that he was on his way. He said to me, "hold her down," and I said that I would. As he turned to go back upstairs, I told him to be careful and he came back and stood in the doorway and asked what I had said, and I told him that I just told him to be careful, and he said, "I always am." Those were the last words that I ever heard him say, as he stood in the doorway, as if to give me one last look at him.

As it turned out, it was good that he did that, as I had to go to the funeral home that had picked up their bodies and make the official identification. I know the papers said Eddy Arnold had made the on-sight identification, but for the life of me I do not see how he could have. A state highway patrolman took Ray Baker and me to Ellis and Kidd Funeral home and Ray told me that he could not go in with me to view the bodies, but that he would wait for me. Mary was sedated and could not go, so I was the one that did it. It's one memory that I wish I could erase, but I'm afraid it's embedded quite firmly.

The funeral home had the bodies mixed up because they had found a wedding band near Dean's remains and thought that he was Jim because they knew Jim was married. Jim did not wear a wedding band; also Jim was wearing what he had on the day he left. He had taken a business suit with him for the meeting, but just wore a blue shirt and blue walking shorts to fly in. They gave me Jim's wallet that they had found (fan James Newberry now has that wallet). I kept it for a month before I finally gave it to Mary. She knew I had it, but did not want to see it just yet. The Governor of Tennessee at that time was Frank Clement and he was wonderful to both Mary and Bobbi Manuel, Dean's wife. He had troopers posted at both places and they were there to do whatever we needed them to do, and when Mary took Jim's body to Carthage, Texas, Governor Clement provided the state plane for the trip.

After hearing that it was believed Jim's plane was down, it was two days before they were found and it was a two-day nightmare for Mary and me and I'm sure it was for Bobbi as well. Many came to the house offering their help and moral support. I can't remember all the ones who came, as I was in a kind of stupor myself, but I do know that Dottie and Bill West were there, as were Chet Atkins and his wife Leona, Billie and Tom Perryman, and Ruth Grammer. Ruth is the wife of Billy Grammer, who had a million-selling record, "Gotta Travel On." She was also my good friend and Mary's. We have done and shared many things together. Ruth, her niece Rita, my Mom and my sister Marsha were part of the search party looking for Jim and Dean. There were others there that were friends both in and out of the music business who came to the house offering to do whatever we needed them to do. Like I said, it was a two-day nightmare and I went 54 hours without any sleep, so I'm a little foggy on just who was there.

We received many telegrams from all over the world from about 60 to 70 different countries sending their condolences and sympathies. I think that is when I realized just what an international artist Jim Reeves truly was.

Mary asked me to go to Texas with them for Jim's funeral and burial there, but I felt that I was needed more at the office and told her that was where I should be. She said that was OK, if I was sure. I'm glad I did stay there at the house because I came down to the office one day shortly after they had left, only to find someone going through our files. He was a songwriter and one that had sold Jim some songs when he was down on his luck. I told him that if he didn't leave that minute that I would call the police and have him arrested. He immediately left and I can't remember ever running into him again. I think that he has since passed away, so I won't mention his name, as he is just not that important. It took a lot of nerve for someone to come into an office and go through the files right after the death of the one who had befriended him.

Mary decided to keep the business going and I agreed to stay on with her, as did Ray Baker for some time after that.

Joyce loves York because..

NASHVILLE and country music met up with historic York when the former secretary of the late singer Jim Reeves paid a visit to the city's Lord Mayor, Coun Malcolm Heppell, a country fan himself.

Joyce Jackson is currently on her first tour of Britain and like Jim Reeves's widow, Mary, 11 years ago, just had to visit the Lord Mayor in the Mansion House.

Highlight

"Mere words can't explain how great it was. The Lord Mayor was so gracious. I loved it. It was the highlight of my visit," she said.

She presented Coun Heppell with a compact disc of Jim Reeves's music.

Yesterday's visit had been arranged by Evening Press reader Derek Cooper, who had sent a book to Joyce many years ago to get the signature of the great singer.

He suggested to David Bussey of Kingsley Drive, Harrogate, who used to run Jim Reeves's

Joyce Jackson, who was personal secretary to Jim Reeves, presents York's Lord Mayor, Coun Malcolm Heppell with a compact disc of Jim's music. Picture by David Varley.

British fan club, that Joyce should follow in Mary Reeves's footsteps and visit York's Lord Mayor.

Now Joyce has vowed to return to North Yorkshire next year when Jim Reeves's fans mark the 25th anniversary of his death with a programme of activities.

With Lord Mayor Coun Malcolm Heppell.

I still miss Jim so much, even after all these years and still sometimes get a knot in my stomach or a lump in my throat when I hear one of his beautiful songs. There was just no one that could deliver a song like Jim could.

Working for and with Jim not only afforded me the opportunity of meeting people in the music industry, but the many fans from all over the world that have visited with us at Jim Reeves Enterprises. Many of these fans and friends have become very special to me. In 1988, Tony Wall from Walsall, England, brought me to his home and we had such a good time. His wife Lena opened their home to me and Tony took me all over the country. I felt so blessed as I got to see England, other than what the tourists see.

Another time in 1989, Tony and many fans and friends from all over England, Norway, Holland and Ireland had me come over again and we met for the 25th anniversary of Jim's passing to pay tribute to him. We met at David Bussey's home in Harrogate, Yorkshire, England. It was a fun time for us all, as we all shared what Jim had meant to each of us. I did several interviews during that time and one such interview became part of a television documentary in London.

When I visited England, I also had the opportunity of meeting with the Lord Mayor of York and presented him with a CD of Jim's music as he was a fan of country music and loved Jim's music. (I'm including a photo of that meeting in this portion.)

Other friends that were fans of Jim's are Mogens and Hanne Jensen of Copenhagen, Denmark. They had written the *Jim Reeves Way* website and told Larry Jordan that they were planning to come to Nashville, and that they wanted to meet me. Larry forwarded their e-mail on to me and I wrote them that I would be happy to meet with them. When we met, there was an instant connection between us, and we have since become more like family than just friends and fans of Jim's. In 2004, they flew Jim's niece, Lani and me over to Copenhagen and truly showed us a trip of a lifetime. They are wonderful and we plan other visits both here and in Denmark. Leo Jackson was also on that same trip with us, but he went on to Oslo, Norway, to do a tour with Arne Benoni, a wonderful Norwegian artist who usually does a tribute to Jim in his shows.

In the early fall of 2007, another fan that I had met earlier in Nashville, came to visit with me in Colorado. Her name is Maggie Buck and she stayed for a week. We had a wonderful time together. I tell about these wonderful friends and fans just to show what an impact Jim did have on the world during his lifetime. It's these people that keep Jim and his music alive causing him to be the "legend" that he deserves to be.

I personally do not feel that Jim has been given the credit that he so richly deserves for pioneering the "country" music that we are hearing today. He wasn't the only one, but he worked so hard at his craft and he wanted it accepted in all homes and with "He'll Have To Go" hitting on all the charts, he attained that goal. Very few have given him credit for opening doors for them so they could become successful. The only person that I personally ever heard thanking Jim for opening the door for him was Vince Gill and I thank Vince for that.

Jim Reeves deserves the title *Legend* as I do not know of many that have been gone 45 years, and still have the fans all over the world that he does. Most everyone still knows who Jim is, and this speaks volumes about his musical legacy.

Jim did a song on a session one time (his last session) that I had asked him to do. It was a song co-written by Dale Noe and Red Sovine titled "Missing You." I'm very thankful that he did that song, as it was and is one of my favorites, though it wasn't released as a single in Jim's lifetime, but posthumously in 1972, and it became another Top 10 record for him. Like the title of the song says, Jim, there hasn't been a year since you've been gone that I haven't been "Missing You."

"THIS GENTLE MAN CALLED JIM"
By JOYCE GRAY JACKSON, AUGUST 1995

HIS LIFE STARTED OUT LIKE SO MANY OTHERS
IN A RURAL AREA WHEN HE WAS A KID
HE PICKED COTTON, BUT HE HAD A DREAM
AND HE DIDN'T STOP LIKE SOME OF THEM DID

HE HAD A LOVE FOR MUSIC AT AN EARLY AGE
HE ALSO LOVED THE GAME OF BASEBALL
HE BECAME A PITCHER AND THEY SAID HE WAS GOOD
HE MUST HAVE BEEN, 'CAUSE A MAJOR LEAGUE CALLED

HE WAS SIGNED BY THE CARDINALS, THE ST. LOUIS TEAM
AND HE PITCHED SEVERAL YEARS FOR THEM
HIS LEFT LEG WAS INJURED, THROWING A MAN OUT ON FIRST
THIS ENDED THE BASEBALL CAREER FOR JIM

HE THEN TURNED TO HIS LOVE FOR MUSIC
WHERE HE PROVED HE COULD HEADLINE A SHOW
HE HAD MANY HITS AND ONE SOLD A MILLION
I KNOW MOST WILL REMEMBER "HE'LL HAVE TO GO"

THERE WERE OTHERS THAT ALSO BECAME HITS
LIKE "FOUR WALLS," "THE BLIZZARD" AND "ANNA MARIE"
THIS WAS THE RECORD THAT WAS ON THE CHARTS
WHEN I INTERVIEWED WITH JIM AND HE HIRED ME

THAT WAS JANUARY 28TH, NINETEEN FIFTY EIGHT
I REMEMBER IT LIKE IT WAS YESTERDAY
I MET MARY, LEO JACKSON AND I MET THE BROWNS
I WAS OVERWHELMED, BUT IN SUCH A GOOD WAY

THE NEXT DAY I BEGAN AS JIM'S SECRETARY
AND I'VE NEVER REGRETTED ONE DAY WITH HIM
IT WASN'T ALWAYS EASY, BUT THAT'S HOW WORK GOES
YET HE WAS FUN TOO, THIS GENTLEMAN JIM

FOR SIX AND A HALF YEARS WE WORKED TOGETHER
AND I TREASURE EACH ONE OF THOSE YEARS
YET EVEN TODAY WHEN I HEAR HIS SONGS
I CAN'T ALWAYS HOLD BACK A FEW LITTLE TEARS

THIS GENTLE MAN THAT WE KNOW AS JIM
PIONEERED COUNTRY MUSIC THAT WE HEAR TODAY
AND IN MY OPINION HE GETS LITTLE CREDIT
FOR ALL THAT HE DID IN PAVING THEIR WAY

THERE IS ONE ARTIST THAT MENTIONED JIM'S NAME
AND SAID THANKS FOR OPENING MUSICAL DOORS FOR HIM
VINCE GILL IS HIS NAME AND HE HAS WORLD ACCLAIM
MUCH LIKE THIS GENTLE MAN CALLED JIM

JIM HELPED OTHERS THAT WERE IN SOME NEED
HE HAD SO MUCH COMPASSION FOR THEM
HE HAD A GOOD HEART AND DID HIS GOOD DEEDS
THIS GENTLE MAN WE KNOW AS JIM

LIKE THE SWEET OLD LADY IN SAN ANTONE, TEXAS
WHO NEEDED A STEREO AND A NEW TV
AND FOR THE LITTLE BLIND GIRL IN NORTH CAROLINA
A BRAILLE WATCH WAS GIVEN BY GENTLEMAN JIM REEVES

THERE ARE SOME OUT THERE THAT ARE QUICK TO JUDGE
AND IN A WAY I FEEL SORRY FOR THEM
THEY WRITE NEGATIVE STORIES WITHOUT EVER MEETING
THIS GENTLE MAN THAT'S CALLED JIM

SO MANY YEARS HAVE NOW COME AND GONE
SINCE THAT FATAL DAY IN 'SIXTY FOUR
SOME HAVE PAID TRIBUTE TO THIS SPECIAL MAN
NOT JUST FOR HIS MUSIC, BUT FOR WHAT HE STOOD FOR

I LOVED THIS MAN AND STILL MISS HIM TODAY
THERE ARE OTHERS THAT FEEL THE SAME WAY ABOUT HIM
HE WON'T BE FORGOTTEN, WE WILL ALWAYS REMEMBER
THIS GENTLE MAN THAT'S CALLED JIM

I was the secretary to Jim Reeves, until his untimely death in 1964. I remained with Jim Reeves Enterprises, however, for a total of 30-plus years. No one knew Jim in just the way that I did. Our desks were cornered and you just don't work that closely with someone and not get to know the person, the real person, and I get a bit angry when I hear negative things being said or written about a man who deserves to be called the Gentleman that he was. Mary, Jim's wife, now has also gone home to be with the Lord, as of Nov. 11, 1999. I find comfort in knowing that they are together again, as they should be.

My Memories ...

Nashville, Tennessee

Hi,

There are times when type written words seem cold and harsh, mere lines and symbols unable to express ones thoughts...ones feelings. This was such a time for me...but in my files I found a letter written over a year ago about another tragedy..a letter that so beautifully mirrored my thoughts concerning the happenings of the last few days that I would like to share it with you:

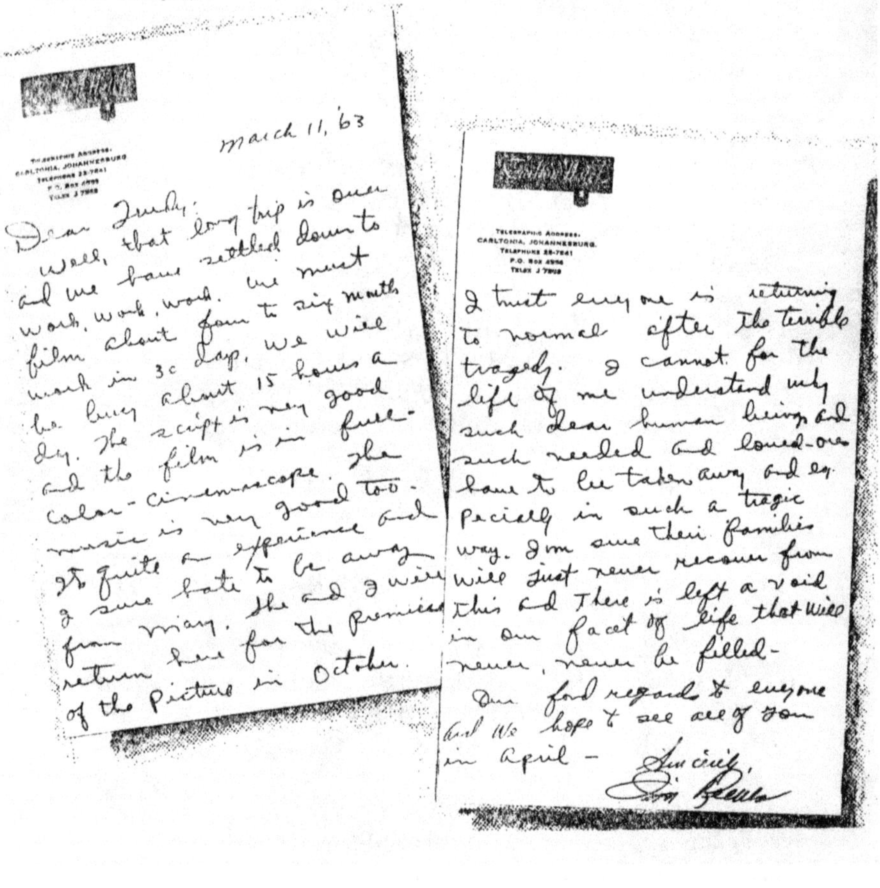

march 11, '63

Dear Judy,

Well, that long trip is over and we have settled down to work, work, work. We must film about four to six months in 30 Day. We will be busy about 15 hours a day. The script is very good and the film is in full color-cinemascope. The music is very good too. It's quite an experience and I sure hate to be away from Mary. She and I will return here for the Premiere of the picture in October.

I trust everyone is returning to normal after the terrible tragedy. I cannot for the life of me understand why such dear human beings and such needed and loved-ones have to be taken away and especially in such a tragic way. I'm sure their families will just never recover from this and There is left a void in our facet of life that will never, never be filled-

Our fond regards to everyone and We hope to see all of you in April -

Sincerely,

Mary and Jim Reeves, shortly after he was awarded a Star of the Year honor, by The Music Reporter.

The Reev-Ettes featured stars such as Dottie West and behind-the-scenes players like Joyce.

Reev-Ettes include Mary Reeves, Kitty Wells, Joyce Jackson, Marti Brown, Dottie West, Vicki, Jackie, Wilma Burgess, Jean Shepard, Ruby Wright, Ginny King, Nell Jackson, Pat Rolfe, Joann Ramsey, Marcie Logan, Janet Slusser, Gail Barnhill, and Minnie Pearl.

At the office: Ray Baker, Joyce and the bossman himself, Jim Reeves.

Jim with he beloved pet Collie, 'Cheyenne.'

Jim records yet another song in RCA's Studio B.   *Jim hears a playback with producer Chet Atkins.*

Jim enjoys a chat with Hank Cochran and Bill Anderson.

Jim & The Blue Boys: Dean Manuel, Leo Jackson, Jim, Mel Rogers and James Kirkland.

Jim & The Blue Boys: Bud Logan, Jimmy Orr, Jim, Dean Manuel and Leo Jackson.

Country legends all: 1st row: Jim, Tex Ritter, Hank Snow, Stuart Hamblen, Eddie Dean, Cousin Herb Henson, Johnny Bond, Squeakin' Deacon (Carl Moore); 2nd row: Tex Williams, Gene King, Dorothy Ritter, Rose Lee Maphis, Joe Maphis, Wade Ray, ShebWooley, Jim Brown, Jimmy Weidner; top row: Hillous Butrum,Chubby Wise, Sleepy McDaniels, Buford Gentry (members of Hank Snow's band).

It was Texas Day at the Jim Reeves Museum. Joining in the celebration were (1st row, from left) Sculptor Bill Rains, Oree Walker (Cindy's mom), Hank Thompson, Floyd Tillman, Olene Tubb (Ernest's wife),Cindy Walker, Tom Perryman, Mary Reeves, Bill Perryman, Billie Perryman (Tom's wife), David Dean, his wife Kitty Dean, Jeanne Pruett and her friend, and Ben Peters; also (top row, from left) Biff Collie, Ernie Ashworth, Jim Ed Brown, Charlie Walker, Justin Tubb, Joe Bob Barnhill, Tommy Hill, and Mary Ann Perryman (Bill's wife).

MARY REEVES...

As I have stated in Jim's story, I met Mary the day that Jim hired me and we became instant friends. I truly loved Mary. She was like a big sister to me and we did many things together before and after Jim's death.

Mary was an avid golfer and one time she took me with her to the Bluegrass Country Club and I played golf with her, but a golfer I'm not! I had fun though. We used to go bowling a great deal. She was an excellent bowler. Ruth Grammer also went bowling with us. She and Mary were on the same bowling team in a league. We all partied together and went dancing and did many fun things.

I will also be grateful that I stayed on with Mary after Jim died. We truly bonded during that tragic time. I stayed with her for a month after Jim's accident. I had lent my apartment to Bill and Tina Walker, who had come from South Africa, with Jim as their sponsor. They never got to do anything with Jim, as they arrived in New York on a Wednesday, and called and talked with Jim, but then he was taken from us on a Friday, and Bill and Tina arrived in Nashville the following Saturday.

I felt that Mary needed me more at that time, so I told them they could use my apartment until they found something. Mary was such a wonderful person and always wanted to do right by all of us. We had get-togethers and Christmas parties and once Mary rented a roller skating rink over in Donelson, Tenn., after hours and we skated for two or three hours.

In 1965, she took all of her staff along with the Blue Boys to Clearwater Beach, Fla., when the Blue Boys were playing the Joyland Club, and doing a live album at the same time. We had such a good time. We went deep sea fishing and our rooms were poolside and we did a lot of swimming, eating, going to the Club at night and just having a wonderful time.

In 1968, she again took her staff along with the Blue Boys to New York City, where the boys were playing The Nashville Room in the Taft Hotel. That was when I met Marlon Brando. Another wonderful time was had by all. Darla Kent Dorris and I went to a couple of plays while there, thanks to the executives at RCA, namely Pat Kelleher who got us wonderful seats. We saw the play "Hair" and "Spofford." Melvyn Douglas starred in "Spofford" and was very good. "Hair" had only been on Broadway for a month at the time we got to see it. It had been playing off-Broadway earlier. We got to see the original cast. The play was very controversial at the time and I suppose rightly so, as there was a total nude scene in it. The last act of the first scene had all the male members of the cast stretched out across the stage during a blackout and then the lights came on and there they stood in the nude. Darla and I had orchestra seats which made us three rows from the stage, so it wasn't hard o figure out why the play was controversial!

Mary was always a joy to be around. She really enjoyed life and had an infectious laugh that just made you feel good. There were times when she should have gotten mad at me, but she didn't. Like one time I put some water on to make a cup of coffee and her neighbor Betty Lewis, yelled for me to come see something outside. Dean Manuel was there also and was on the phone. I forgot about the water in her teakettle and when I came back in the house, there was an awful smell, which I learned was melted metal, as the entire bottom of the teakettle had melted and run into the drip pan of her stove and only missed some electrical wiring by millimeters. I asked Dean could he not smell that - or see it even. He said no, he didn't see or smell anything and he was in our den office right next to the kitchen! It was a good heavy-duty aluminum teakettle. Mary and Jim were out of town and I had to get another drip pan and then they got back in town, so I showed Mary the teakettle and told her what I had done. She just laughed! We didn't tell Jim for quite some time, but he also thought it was funny. The teakettle had been a wedding gift to them.

Then there was the time when again they were out of town and I was staying at the house. Jim always wanted me to stay in their room when they were gone, as they had a phone in their bedroom. This was when our office was in the den. They had just bought a new bedroom suite, maybe a couple of weeks earlier, and I smoked at the time. I had gone to bed, but around midnight I heard the office phone in the den ringing, and was afraid not to answer it because I thought it might be them calling. It was a DJ from Canada, Loren Harasen. I had put my cigarette in an ashtray on the dresser near the bed when I heard the phone. By the time I had finished the conversation, which was quite lengthy, I might add, the cigarette had fallen out of the ashtray, onto the dresser, burning a place about an inch to an inch-and-a-half long on their new dresser.

There's more! I used to sew some for Mary and did some altering of her clothes. Well, I was to alter this beautiful silk dress and had it in my sewing room. I was cleaning a head of lettuce one evening, using a surgical steel-bladed knife to take out the core, when it slipped, cutting my left thumb pretty badly. My daughter Joy ran into the sewing room to find something to wrap around it, and she cut a big strip out of that beautiful silk dress. I was sick about it and hated to tell Mary what had happened, but when I did, she told me to tell Joy not to worry about it, that she had done a good thing in trying to help me, and if that was the worst thing that ever happened to her, then she would get along just fine. That's the kind of person Mary Reeves was! Is it any wonder why I loved her so much? Like I said, she was not only my boss, but more like a big sister and friend. We even double-dated on several occasions. It was on one of these double-dates that I met singer Johnny Duncan (of "Thinkin' Of a Rendezvous" fame). We had specifically gone to Bowling Green to catch his act. We started having Fan Fair back in 1972 (see photos of our Fan Fair booths) and they were always a lot of fun. I think they have changed the name now to CMA Music Festival or something like that. I don't remember the exact year that we began having softball tournaments, but it might have been 1975 or 1976. Mary had a team and she called them Mary Reeves' Reev-Ettes. During the time they started having these tournaments, we never lost a game, not one! We got a huge trophy, after five years of winning, which Mary displayed in the Jim Reeves Museum. I suppose that went by the wayside like all the other memorabilia did when everything was sold out from under Mary, after she became ill.

I was the catcher for the team and we had stars like Dottie West, Minnie Pearl and Kitty Wells on our team. What fun we all had. That's when I learned that Barbara Mandrell was sometimes not a very good sport. She was a sore loser, but always got the big headlines, because of who she was, and Mary's team would get the little notification of how we had won the tournament. Barbara didn't have her own team in the beginning, but played on ABC-DOT Records' Dot's Hot Shots. Barbara later formed her own team, The Do-Rites. She always came in second and we always won. I guess she felt she should have won. Sorry, but we got the trophy!

Mary was such a classy lady and fit into any group of people by just being Mary. She was always friendly with everyone and made you feel like you were the one most important to her, and she was this way until she started getting ill. I could see changes in her as early as 1993. In August 1995, there was a memorial for Jim in Carthage, Texas, in which Mary was presented a huge plaque depicting Jim's many hit recordings, and at that time she was very ill. The doctors had said she had Pernicious Anemia, which was allegedly brought about from being among so many cats and even being scratched and bitten by them.

By this time, her second husband Terry Davis had over 100 cats in the house that they lived in. I know that Human Services had to be called on several occasions to try and either get her removed, or to get rid of the cats, as they were allegedly causing her illness. She had flown to Carthage, but her clothing had such an odor from all the cats that Billie Perryman had to give her an outfit to put on, so she could be presentable to the public, and I went to her room to put makeup on her, and had to have the door open to let fresh air in, as the cat odor was almost unbearable. This was so sad to all of us who loved her, and it wasn't long after her return from Carthage that she was placed in a nursing home, diagnosed with Dementia or Alzheimer's. I'm not a doctor, but I personally believe all of this was brought on by the cats and the lack of treatment she received from her second husband. So very sad.

While she was in the first nursing home, she was still able to be taken out by her husband for lunch, etc,, and while doing so on one occasion, she fell and broke her hip, prompting her placement in Vanderbilt Hospital. I went to see her there, as I did when she was in the nursing homes, even though I no longer worked for her. She was still my friend and I still loved her. She did not know or remember everyone that came to see her, but she always remembered me and would always call me by my name, and this assured me that she did know who I was.

Mary was so good to all of us and her passing left such a void in my life. I had lost a former boss, a friend, a big sister and so much more, all rolled up into one beautiful lady. I loved you so much Mary, and I pray you and Jim are again enjoying being with each other as you should be.

Joyce with Doris Gath, then Jim Reeves Fan Club vice president, admiring a Jim Reeves album release. At right we see Reev-Ettes Mary Reeves and Minnie Pearl.

After winning for five straight years, a big trophy was given. We won the trophy! We're #1!

Catcher Joyce Jackson awaits a fly ball.

Reev-Ettes team players: Ruby Wright Taylor, Marsha Basore, Kitty Wells and Joyce Jackson.

Joyce and Mary in their cowgirl hats at Fan Fair.

Kitty Wells and Mary Reeves, Reev-Ettes!

Mary Reeves managed the Reeves legacy.

Bringing in another home run!

At the office: Joyce, Darla Kent Dorris and Mary.

Leo and Bud Logan performing in the Nashville Room at the Taft Hotel in New York.

Party time for Mary (from left), Bunky Keels, Joyce, Darla; and (standing) Bud and Margaret Colburn.

Leo, Mary, Darla, Bud and Joyce clowning around at the office.

Jim and his Blue Boys (from left) Bobby Dyson, Mel Rogers, Jim, Leo Jackson and Dean Manuel.

Mary and Joyce at a DJ Convention.   *Mary, Joyce and Darla during DJ Convention.*

*Mary Reeves after having her first
haircut in eight years, Aug. 22, 1978.*

*Darla, Margaret Colburn, Joyce, Bunky, Mary, Bud
and Ginny King. We gals were all wearing paper
dresses at this particular DJ Convention!*

*Mary with Tony Wall and
David Bussey. David was
Reeves' English Fan Club pres-
ident for some 25 years.*

The very first Jim Reeves Enterprises Fan Fair Booth,
1972, staffed by Ginny King and Joyce Jackson.

A few years later, another Jim Reeves Enterprises Fan Fair Booth
boasted a cardboard Mary Reeves out front, with Joyce on the job.

CHET ATKINS...

I first met Chet right after I began working for Jim Reeves. Chet was Jim's A&R Director (that's what they were called back then). By back then, I am referring to the late 1950's. Chet was always a quiet, reserved man and one that was very hard to get to know. In fact, I never did get to know him very well, yet I knew him for some 43 years.

There was a period of time when I maintained the promotion department for Jim Reeves Enterprises and Shannon Records on the third floor of the RCA Building. This was during the late 1960's and early '70's through July 1975. Chet was head of RCA Nashville by then; however, he left his post as RCA head during the above-mentioned period of time, yet maintained offices in the RCA Building on the third floor next to mine. Jerry Bradley, son of the renowned producer Owen Bradley, then became RCA Nashville's Director.

It was during this time that I feel I finally got to know Chet a little better. We had lunch together on many occasions and there were times that I would just go in and visit with him. His secretary at the time, Carolyn Campbell, would always let me know if he was with someone or if he was too busy to see me. When I did visit, the main subject would be about Jim Reeves and/or some project that he was working on, but he always treated me with respect, and he was never so busy that he refused to see me if I asked for some time.

I had the opportunity to meet many people that I would have never met, had I not had my office next to Chet's. Chet introduced me to Perry Como, another very nice quiet-spoken man and one, of course, that was extremely talented. One of my very favorite Perry Como songs was entitled "You're Just in Love." Then there was Homer & Jethro (Jethro Burns and Chet were brothers-in-law, since Chet's wife Leona and Jethro's wife Lois were twin sisters). There was a time when they were one of the funniest comedy duos that country music ever had! Chet introduced me to Jethro, also a great mandolinist. One day I was coming out of my office and ran into Chet and Merle Travis (Merle was no doubt one of the most renowned guitar stylists of our time). These are just a few of the people that stand out the most in my memory. They are *greats* that have contributed so much to our music industry.

There were times that I would become involved with various charities and whenever I would ask Chet for either a donation or an article of something personal of his for a celebrity auction, he never once refused me.

Chet was such a vital part of Jim's recording career and because of that many have wanted to interview him regarding his and Jim's working association. I set up several of these interviews with people from England, South Africa and many other parts of the world. He never refused me the time to spend with these people.

Over the years Chet has received awards for about everything the music industry has to offer, but I believe that one of the ones that he was the proudest of was the Humanitarian Association of Christians and Jews Award. I was fortunate enough to attend the festivities. What a thrill for me to watch Chet being given this award.

I will never forget how sweet Chet was when we knew that it was Jim that went down in that terrible plane crash. He along with several others came to Mary's and Jim's house to extend their personal sympathies and share their feelings of mutual loss with us. Some of the others that come to mind were the executives from the RCA New York office. They didn't just send messages of sympathy, they came to Nashville personally, and when Mary took Jim to be buried near Carthage, these New York executives cared enough about me, Jim's secretary, to take me to dinner, so that I would not be alone. As stated earlier, I had chosen to remain in Nashville to take care of the office and handle the business affairs rather than go to Texas with Mary. We had already had a Prayer Service for him in Nashville, and felt someone should stay and maintain the Enterprises office. Some of the executives were Harry Jenkins, RCA Vice President (he came to work with us at Jim Reeves Enterprises after he retired from RCA). Harry passed away a few years ago, but we all surely loved Harry. Then there was Pat Kelleher, always one of my favorite people, not only at RCA, but period. He was the one that I talked with the most in New York while working for Jim, and he never failed to show he cared. Even after Jim got killed, Pat would still give me a call from time-to-time and whenever he came to Nashville, always took me to dinner. I'll never forget Vito Blando, promotion director in New York, who later went to Atlanta. What a nut! He was full of bull, but so much fun. There was always a good time when Vito was around.

George Parkhill always seemed a bit on the gruff side, but really was a big ol' pussycat. Nashville's promotion man at the time was Bob Holt and, of course, Bob is the one responsible for my getting the job with Jim in the first place. I don't want to forget

Ray Clark, one of the kindest, most gentle men that I ever had the pleasure of knowing.

I don't think Chet would mind sharing this space with the gentlemen that I have mentioned. It just seems appropriate somehow to bring them into the picture at this time, especially since they were all working associates of Chet's. They were a wonderful group of people and I just don't feel that the big companies of today have the compassion for others that they had back then. I'll just bet you'll agree. I would not take anything for my having known you all those years Chet, and I'll keep some of the secrets that I know you want kept . . . I'll keep everyone wondering, OK?

Country Music Hall of Famer Chet Akins, great guitarist, an architect of the *Nashville Sound,* RCA honcho, my friend and a super nice guy, passed away June 30, 2001.

FARON YOUNG ...

Faron was known as the *Young Sheriff* for most of his music career, having starred in a movie by that title. I first met Faron in 1954, when he came to Louisville, along with the Wilburn Brothers. They were part of his show at that time. I didn't get to know him then, but I was a member of his fan club, which was run by Shirley Valliere of Flint, Mich. She later moved to Nashville and became his and Hubert Long's secretary.

Hubert was Faron's manager and booking agent. In 1957, I made my first trip to Nashville and went to Faron's office at Shirley's invitation, and was able to visit with Shirley, Faron and Hubert. Shirley was getting out a Fan Club Journal and I volunteered to help with it, turning down a trip to Memphis to visit Elvis Presley. Gordon Terry, who also used to work for Faron as his fiddle player, knew Elvis and asked if I wanted to go. I told him that I had promised Shirley that I would help her. There was a girl from Minnesota, Sharon Begin, who took Gordon up on the invitation. She later told me she had a wonderful visit and that Elvis was great! In many ways, I have regretted not going, but I did get to know Faron better.

I recall one evening after the *Friday Night Frolics,* I was coming down on the only elevator in the building and Faron was on it, along with some jerk whom neither of us knew, and he began flirting with me and saying some rather off-color remarks. Faron told him off in no uncertain terms and the guy apologized to both me and Faron. Faron was a good friend of Jeanie and Frank Oakley's, and I got to know him even better through them. Jim and Faron were also good friends and he used to come by the office once in a while to visit with Jim. One day he was telling Jim about something this person had done to him and said, "I told him he could stick a fork in his a— 'cause he was done." that's the first time I had ever heard anyone say that. I've heard it many times since then.

During my early years in Nashville, there were a lot of parties at first one person's house, then another's. Hillous and Phyllis Butrum used to have parties at their house all the time. Hillous was one of Hank Williams' original Drifting Cowboys. One night during one of their parties, Faron and Mattie George got into an argument about something or the other and Mattie slapped Faron. He did nothing at that time, but she went around bragging about how she had slapped Faron and she would do it again. She did, and when she did that time, Faron back-handed her, knocking her down. Someone grabbed him because he was very angry, but rightly so. In my opinion, she deserved it. Ralph Emery was there that night, along with Doyle Wilburn, Grady Martin (one of Nashville's leading guitarists, who later went to work for Willie Nelson), and many other behind-the-scenes people were also there.

There is a Nashville organization called R.O.P.E. (Reunion Of Professional Entertainers) of which I am charter member #65. Faron was also a member and had entertained many times for ROPE, as well as just attending the festivities. It was started by Gordon Terry and the main reason for ROPE was to build a retirement home for musicians/entertainers and those of us who have worked in the business, if we cannot afford a place when we reach our golden years.

Many people knew Faron much better than I did, but I am glad that I got to know him as much as I did. He was very talented and I don't feel he came close to reaching his potential as an artist, writer or actor. Most everyone who listens to country music remember Faron's many hits like "Goin' Steady," "If You Ain't Lovin' (You Ain't Livin')," "Alone With You," "It's Four in the Morning," and of course the Willie Nelson-penned "Hello Walls," just a few of his many smash recordings.

My brother-in-law, Stu Basore, was part of Faron's band for a while and did quite a bit of traveling around the country with him. He could tell you some Faron Young stories I'm sure. There are *many* Faron Young stories and I'll just bet a portion of most of them are true.

Faron told me one time that he would walk a mile to see Hank Snow drunk. He said one time that they were in a suite during one of the conventions and Hank had a pipe in his hand and was trying to hit his mouth with it, which Faron said he never did make, because he looked over at Faron, who was laughing his head off. When Hank realized this, he stopped trying to smoke his pipe and said, "Did you see that Faron, wasn't that funny?" I think you would have had to know both Faron and Hank to get the picture of just how funny this was, at least to Faron.

He was full of himself, but I sure did think a lot of Faron, and he always treated me with respect and showed me that he cared about me as a friend. In the 1990's, he got really sick and had to be on oxygen, causing him to stay at home and not go around people, which was very depressing for him, as he was a people person. On Dec. 10, 1996, Faron ended his life and the music industry lost one of its greatest entertainers, as he not only sang great, but truly entertained an audience. I sure do miss you, Sheriff.

My Memories ...

Faron and Joyce backstage.

Faron and Joyce away from the Opry.

*Joyce and Shirley Valliere Johnson,
Faron's personal secretary.*

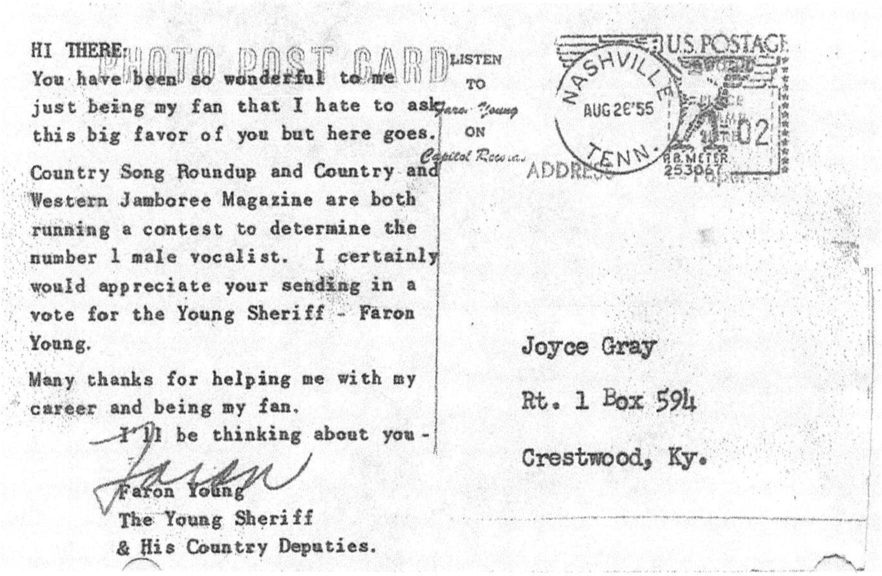

HI THERE:
PHOTO POST CARD
You have been so wonderful to me just being my fan that I hate to ask this big favor of you but here goes.

Country Song Roundup and Country and Western Jamboree Magazine are both running a contest to determine the number 1 male vocalist. I certainly would appreciate your sending in a vote for the Young Sheriff - Faron Young.

Many thanks for helping me with my career and being my fan.

I'll be thinking about you -

Faron

Faron Young
The Young Sheriff
& His Country Deputies.

LISTEN TO Faron Young ON Capitol Records

U.S. POSTAGE
NASHVILLE AUG 26'55 TENN.
02
P.B. METER 253067
ADDRESS

Joyce Gray
Rt. 1 Box 594
Crestwood, Ky.

A postcard from Faron at the height of his career.

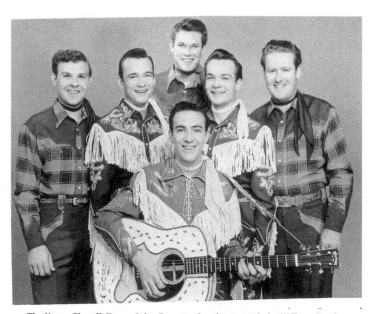

The Young Sheriff, Faron & his Deputies bandsmen, with the Wilburn Brothers.

GOVERNOR JIMMIE DAVIS...

Many of you will know Jimmie Davis and some won't, but I know all of you are familiar with the song "You Are My Sunshine," co-written by Jimmie Davis (with Charles Mitchell). This was only one of his many accomplishments, however, as he was twice Governor of Louisiana, and lived a rich, full life until his death at age 101 on Nov. 5, 2000.

He became a friend of David McCormick, who owns the Ernest Tubb Record Shops in Nashville; Fort Worth, Texas; And Pigeon Forge, Tenn.; and the Texas Troubadour Theatre (near the Opryland area). I worked for David from October 1992 to April 1995, in the mail order department downtown on Lower Broad. While with David, we had a get-together honoring Gov. Jimmie Davis. Many came to tell how he had touched their lives and shared their memories with us, but one person in particular that he helped to guide was Dottie Rambo, who paid such a lovely tribute to him. (Dottie was killed in a bus accident in May 2008). I felt so honored to be a part of that wonderful evening.

When Gov. Davis turned 94 years of age, David once again honored him by having his birthday celebration in the Green Room at WSM's *Grand Ole Opry*. It took place during the Opry show and all its members were invited to participate. I was once again blessed to be a part of the event, and even more thrilled to have the rare privilege of making his 94th birthday cake. I will always treasure the memory of having met and played a small part in the life of this Country Music Hall of Famer. Having enjoyed classic country cuts like "Nobody's Darlin' But Mine" and "There's a New Moon Over My Shoulder," plus yet another career in gospel music, Jimmie Davis was truly an icon in the music industry.

JUMPIN' BILL CARLISLE...

I wouldn't trade having known "Jumpin" Bill Carlisle for anything in the world. This man was a priceless piece of work. I loved him dearly. I really don't know how to start telling about him, but I'll just start with the fact that he was a fixture on the *Grand Ole Opry* for many, many years, singing his hits like "Too Old to Cut the Mustard," 'No Help Wanted," "Knothole" and "Is Zat You, Myrtle?" He sang about half of a song then about midway through it, he'd jump up and down a few times. The audience loved it.

Bill loved the NASCAR races and many times he and musician-songwriter George Riddle would go over to (Patsy Cline's widower) Charlie Dick's house to watch it. I joined them on several occasions. On one of these occasions, I told Bill I needed to get me another car and he said he had one for sale. It was a little bronze Toyota Tercel SR 5. I went to look at it and decided that I liked it, so I bought it. The turn signal lever was broken and when I brought this to Bill's attention, he said it wouldn't cost much to repair it and that he would knock $25 off the selling price. I said OK, but then it cost me $87 to get the lever repaired, and when I told Bill this, he said that the car was in much better condition now and he hadn't charged me enough. The car also backfired quite a bit and we all had a good time with that, and Bill thought he should also charge more for the car since it was bringing us so much pleasure! He was such fun. What a sense of humor.

The infamous Toyota Joyce bought.

I'll never forget when Dottie West died. Charlie Dick, Bill, my two sisters, Glenda and Marsha, and I went to the funeral home for visitation. When we were ready to leave, Bill said he'd buy us all dinner and told Charlie to pull into the White Castle. Charlie did and we all ate White Castle hamburgers on Bill. Now out here in Colorado, I have to buy frozen White Castles, but when I do, I can't help but think of Bill. What a riot he was!

Bill died at the age of 94 on March 17, 2003. He may have been 94 years old, but Bill, you were so young at heart. I loved you so much and you were so much fun to be around. I miss you and that infectious smile that always led to out-and-out laughter.

ERNEST TUBB...

Although I knew Ernest Tubb mainly through working at Jim Reeves Enterprises, I did know his son Justin Tubb quite well. I'm including his own story in this book. I also became good friends with Ernest's daughter Elaine. She and I worked together at the Ernest Tubb Record Shop.

Many times I would go to the WSM *Midnight Jamboree* at the Ernest Tubb Record Shop on Broadway, and was always allowed backstage. Ernest was so nice to everyone. He gave Loretta Lynn her first big national radio exposure on his *Jamboree,* the first day she was in town. I believe it was Teddy and Doyle Wilburn who brought her to the shop and introduced her to Ernest, and gave up one of their spots on the show, so she could do a song.

When Ernest celebrated his Golden Anniversary in Show Business, they gave him a 50-year ring, which was very unique. When Bill Rains was commissioned to do a sculpture of Ernest during one of the latter Fan Fairs, "E.T." was in his booth about two booths down from where we had the Jim Reeves Enterprises' booth, and Bill wanted to get a good look at the ring Ernest had received. He wanted it to be a part of the sculpture and asked me how he could get a good peek at it, and perhaps even take a picture of it (Bill and I are great friends). Bill said he did not want to interrupt him, as he was talking with fans and having his picture made with them. I told him I would go ask Ernest if we could look at his ring. I went up to Ernest and told him that Bill needed to have a good look at his ring for the sculpture that he was to make, and Ernest just took that ring off his finger and gave it to me. I still don't know if he knew who he was giving it to. I took it back to our booth and Bill photographed it and then I took it back to Ernest and thanked him. He put it back on his finger and never stopped talking to his fans. One of E.T.'s song titles was inscribed on the back of his guitar: "Thanks A Lot."

I was fortunate enough to attend the funeral services for Ernest (who died on Sept. 6, 1984), where Cal Smith (once one of Ernest's Texas Troubadours) and country-pop crossover artist B.J. Thomas sang some of Ernest's favorite songs.

I wonder how many other artists have either recorded or sung on stage the classic E.T. standard "Walking the Floor Over You"? This was his 1941 million-selling signature song and a #20 pop single in those pre-country chart days; and I loved the way he and

Red Foley did "Too Old To Cut the Mustard."

Ernest was inducted into the Country Music Hall of Fame in 1965. A true stylist and one most copied by many in the music industry. Wish I could have known you better, Ernest. Thanks a lot!

TEX RITTER...

I first met Tex Ritter during the time when he co-hosted the all-night WSM radio show with Ralph Emery, but got to know him better during the time that my office was in the RCA Building. Tex and his son Tommy came by every once in a while and we would just sit and visit. I loved these times and was honored to be able to hear many wonderful stories that Tex shared. I had been a fan of both Tex and his horse, White Flash, from the western movies that he was in, so you can imagine how thrilled I was to really get to know this cowboy. I know he was also my sister Glenda's favorite cowboy film star. She also got to meet him during one of the DJ Conventions.

When Tex was inducted into the Texas Country Music Hall of Fame (the same year that Jim Reeves was also inducted) in 1998, I participated in all the festivities. Willie Nelson, Gene Autry, Joe Allison (co-writer of Jim's "He'll Have to Go") and Cindy Walker (who wrote Jim's #1 "Distant Drums") were also inducted this same year. Allison also co-wrote Tex's Top Five 1946 single "When You Leave, Don't Slam the Door."

While backstage chatting with Willie Nelson, Tommy Ritter came up to me and asked if I remembered him? He had moved away from Nashville for many years by then (and had become a lawyer). I told him that, of course, I did; how could I forget all those wonderful times he and his dad had come by. I was afraid he would not remember me, but he did and we chatted for a little while, just talking and remembering some of the fun times when they visited our office. It wasn't long until John Ritter came over to Tommy, who introduced me to him and we talked for a while. Tommy told John that I had worked for Jim and that we met when he and their dad stopped by my office one day. John was so nice and friendly and happy to learn that I felt honored by the visits from his brother and father. (John starred in the TV sitcoms *Three's Company* and *8 Simple Rules for Dating My Teenage Daughter,* prior to his death on Sept. 11, 2003.)

Tex, in my opinion, was a great man, not only in stature, but also as a pioneer of western music in song and in the movies, and I know he was a wonderful family man because his two songs reflected this. I also had the pleasure of meeting Tex's wife and John and Tommy's mother, Dorothy Ritter, herself a former screen star. She was indeed a wonderful lady. I would never have had the pleasure of meeting John had it not been for Tommy and for this I truly thank him. What an honor to have met and been able to be around this family.

Tex Ritter was inducted into the Country Music Hall of Fame in 1964, and the Nashville Songwriters' Hall of Fame in 1971. Tex died on Jan. 2, 1974.

RED FOLEY ...

My meeting with Red was brief, but what a pleasure and what a treasure it was to have done so! It was in Atlanta, Ga. Several were there for the Atlanta NASCAR race and for the big country and western show that always took place on Saturday night prior to the Sunday race event.

Red was on the show along with Jim Ed Brown and the Wilburn Brothers, Teddy and Doyle. Charlie Dick was also there. I'm sure there were others on the show, but I can't recall just who. At any rate, the race was rained out. I don't know just how many of these NASCAR races that I have tried to see, but to date haven't seen one, because it always rained whenever and wherever I went, so I quit going.

On Sunday morning, most of us had gathered at the Air Host Inn, so we could either catch a plane back to Nashville or just so we could have a little fun, despite the race being rained out. I know I was to ride back with Jim Ed, which I did. Most of the artists were staying at the motel anyway and this is where I met Red Foley. Marijohn Wilkin, co-writer of "Waterloo" (along with John D. Loudermilk), also had a room there, and since we were friends, she invited me to come by her room and have breakfast with her. We had just ordered breakfast when Red came by. He'd had a few drinks, but was not drunk. He was just in a good mood and very funny. He asked if anyone wanted to run a footrace around the swimming pool with him. No one said anything, so I told him I would. Red wasn't physically able to run, so we just trotted all the way around the pool.

I never hear his name without recalling that Sunday morning and the race around the swimming pool. I'll just bet that I am the only person who has ever done that with Red. What a great voice this man had, with such standards as "Peace in the Valley," "Chattanoogie Shoe Shine Boy" and "Old Shep." Red also emceed the network portion of the *Grand Ole Opry* for several years, sponsored by Prince Albert Tobacco. I don't know just when he left the Opry, but I do know that he also had his own TV show called *The Ozark Jubilee* (later called *Jubilee USA*) and in 1958, when he had to go into the hospital for a couple of months, Jim Reeves was asked to take his place, which he did.

Red also made a series of duet records with my friend Kitty Wells, including the #1 "One By One" in 1954. Pat Boone is married to Red's daughter, Shirley.

Red died Sept. 19, 1968, silencing one of the greatest voices in my opinion, that the music industry has ever had. He was elected to the Country Music Hall of Fame in 1967. How fondly I remember Red and I'm thankful we met. I wouldn't have missed it for the world.

MERLE HAGGARD ...

Songwriter Hank Cochran first introduced me to Merle Haggard, somewhere around the late 1960's. I can't remember just how or where, but I do know that I enjoyed his singing and songwriting very much, and he was so easy to look at!

When the Songwriters' Association was formed, their first banquet was held at the Holiday Inn-Vanderbilt in Nashville. Merle attended, as did most of the songwriters of that era. I think all of us at Jim Reeves Enterprises were there. We usually went to all the various functions during convention time.

Either I wasn't looking where I was going or Merle wasn't looking where he was going, I don't know which, but all of a sudden I found myself on the floor. Merle ran smack into me and literally knocked me down! This wasn't too long after I had first met him, and he still remembered my name. He reached down to help me up and apologized. I remember saying to him that he could knock me down anytime ... I wasn't hurt and we had a good laugh.

The next time I met Merle, he was in town doing the Porter Wagoner TV show. He was then married to Bonnie Owens, who had once been Mrs. Buck Owens. Hank Cochran and I had dinner that same night with Dick Curless (one of our industry's most beautiful - and most overlooked - voices) and we planned to meet with Merle and Bonnie after the filming was complete. We were to meet at a place in Nashville's Printer's Alley called The Captain's Table. Buck Trent (a fantastic banjo player and then a regular on Porter's show) and his wife Pat also joined us. I remember that I was so sleepy from being up the night before, and Merle gave me some kind of pill (an upper) to wake me up and all it did was make me sleepier. Hank got mad at me because I kept nodding and tried to prop my head up, but my chin kept slipping off my hand. Hank finally gave up and took me home.

As the years passed, I would see Merle from time-to-time at one function or another. Then one day, while I was still at Jim Reeves Enterprises, I looked out the window of my office and pulling up in front was a police car. I wondered why they were coming to our office. Then Glen Martin (another songwriter), got out of the police car and was closely followed by none other than Merle Haggard. They came into my office and the policeman went on his way. (This policeman was Paul Scurry, who was killed a few years later in the line of duty.) This had me somewhat curious. I asked Glen what in the world they were doing and he told me they had run out of gas on the Interstate, which was about two miles or so away and that the policeman was nice enough to pick them up, while they were walking. He told the policeman that he knew me and would appreciate it if he would take them to my office. He wanted to know if I could help them out by getting them some gas and taking them back to the car. Seems they had borrowed Ronnie Reno's van and Ronnie had give them $10 to put gas in the van, but they forgot to do so. Merle had the flu and didn't feel well and they were on their way to Glen's house, so he could rest and get better. As fate would have it, I just happened to have a gas can in my little Volkswagen because I needed to get gas for my lawn mower. So I loaded up Glen and Merle, we got the gas, and I took them to the van and stayed long enough to make sure the van started and saw them on their way.

Merle is one of the most-copied artists today. So many have been influenced by his style of singing. However, and this is only my opinion, Merle's particular styling seems to have been fashioned after Lefty Frizzell. It really doesn't matter because I enjoy listening to them both and again Merle, you can knock me down anytime you want. I'm so glad we bumped into each other.

Clint Black, who recorded with Roy in 1991, could have passed for his son.

ROY ROGERS ...

Back in the 1950's, Roy Rogers and Dale Evans had a TV show which they always signed off with singing "Happy Trails," written by Dale. I know many will remember those Saturday afternoon shows as I do. A lot of kids looked up to these people as heroes. I know I did. I never dreamed that I would one day meet my TV hero, but some 25 years later, I did.

I was in a bowling league called The Music Business Mixed League. We always bowled on Sunday at 8:30 p.m., which meant it wasn't over most of the time until around 11. Because of having to work the next day and getting through so late, some of us would go to the bowling alley with our hair rolled up with a scarf tied around it. Now I know you are beginning to get the picture and you're right!

I had just joined the other members of my particular team, hair all rolled up with that stupid scarf tied around the curlers, when I looked over at the team bowling on the lanes next to ours and there he was . . . My Saturday Afternoon Hero! I could have just died right then and there! If there had been a way for me to have gotten on that bowling ball, I would have, and just rolled right out of sight.

Roy had come with songwriter Charlie Craig and he was subbing for one of Charlie's team members. Charlie properly introduced him to me and all I could think of was my hair being in those darn rollers. I apologized for the way I looked and tried to explain why I came that way . . .God, I was embarrassed! He was so nice and said he was there to bowl, not to look at people's hair.

It turned out to be one of the most fun evenings that I have ever had at that bowling alley. Roy was real and so much fun. He was a good bowler, too. I just left my hair up and we all made a big joke about it and kept on bowling. What a thrill it was for me to find out that my Saturday afternoon TV hero was also that great in person.

This has been a memory that I have treasured and shared many times and it's still fun to think about and funny to tell again and again.

Thank you, Roy Rogers for being such a nice cowboy.

Incidentally, Roy was the only person inducted twice into the Country Music Hall of Fame, first in 1980 as an Original Member of the Sons of the Pioneers, and on his own in 1988. Roy Rogers died on July 6, 1998, at age 86.

DOTTIE WEST ...

Dottie West and I go back to 1961, when she was still married to Bill West, the songwriter and guitarist, and they'd moved back to Tennessee from Ohio, to a 600-acre farm, near Nashville. This was even before Dale, her youngest, was born.

I spent a great deal of time with Dottie and her family out at that old farm house and these are memories that I am happy I have, but they do need sharing.

We sat one night at her kitchen table and wrote a song. It even got recorded and released, but only in Canada. The artist was a boy named Larry Lee and the song was called "Stood Up." We had to change the title when we reported it to BMI, so they would not get it confused with the big hit of the same title by Ricky Nelson. So we then called ours "I Can't Stand To Be Stood Up." When the record came out it only had "Stood Up" as the title. I think my grand total earnings was $14. That was enough to establish me as a professional writer! I've often wondered if the writer of Ricky Nelson's song got our royalties.

I remember many times when a whole group of us would be out at Dottie's and usually I would spend the entire weekend. I know one night she asked me to stay and I didn't have any extra clothes with me, so Roger Miller, one of those out there jamming, said he'd take me back to my apartment to pick up a change of clothes (I didn't have a car then). On the way during our conversation, Roger said something I will always treasure. He said, "Joyce, when I see you, I see a lady." I didn't know what to say. I hope I said *thank you.*

Roger, like myself, was at the West's house a great deal of the time when he was in town. I remember one night just Roger and I were there and again in Dottie's kitchen (we spent a lot of time at her kitchen table). She and I asked Roger if he could write a song about whatever we might ask him to write. He assured us he could and did! It didn't matter what we mentioned, a door, a lamp, stove, table or anything else that might be in the room or in our minds, he'd write at least four lines and each one would have a different melody. I was so impressed and still am where Roger and his talent are concerned. I'm honored and proud that he was my friend.

By this time, Dottie had become friends with Patsy Cline. Patsy and I were also friends. Patsy was good to Dottie in many ways. Dottie was just breaking into the Nashville scene and Patsy offered a lot of advice in different aspects of the music business. That was Patsy. She did the same for Loretta Lynn. So many artists seem to be jealous of another's success, but not her. She was always there with the big push and I loved that about Patsy.

It wasn't long after Patsy died that Dottie and Bill moved to East Nashville. It was during this time that Dottie's and my friendship really grew. I was at her house even more than before, as she was living closer. On Friday nights, we'd play Canasta. Charlie Dick and I would go to Dottie and Bill's for Canasta. Dottie and I always partnered against Charlie and Bill, and I suppose it's a toss-up as to who won the most games. It didn't really matter, as it was such fun, and now a wonderful memory. It was at their house that Justin Tubb wrote "Love is No Excuse" that Dottie recorded with Jim Reeves (her first Top 10). What a great blending of voices!

Speaking of Jim, he was instrumental in helping Dottie get her RCA contract. He truly believed in her as a writer and singer, and he wasn't wrong. It was about this time that Justin and Dottie, and I don't remember just who all was involved, instigated the nicknaming of many of us. I know that Justin nicknamed Dottie, Beulah! She was Beulah to some of us from then on. Justin was Proctor and I was Gladys!

Thinking of Justin reminds me of a time he and Dottie were booked on the same show in Illinois. I believe they had to play both Freeport and Rockford. Dottie asked me to go along, so people wouldn't talk about her. I went and now I'm so glad that I shared such a special weekend with Dottie and Justin.

Dottie and I shopped, cooked, laughed, cried and did about everything together that friends do. I had my last talk and cry with her about two weeks before the horrible accident that took her from us. She told me many things that day. She was devastated by all the adverse things happening to her that year. I feel she could and would have handled the IRS tax problems and come out on top from all the stress they were putting her through. But her heart was hurt, because she had found out who told the IRS where some of her personal belongings were stored and they were supposed to be her friends. She knew they had received a good sum of money for the information. She cried her heart out to me about them. She was totally crushed, but I don't think even they could have kept her down, because she assured me that she would come back, and she had several projects she was already working on.

Dottie was also beginning to write again. She was the first country female to receive a Grammy award. It was for her 1964 hit "Here Comes My Baby," which she co-wrote with Bill.

She appeared in the 1965 movie "Second Fiddle To A Steel Guitar." Several of the girl country singers, including Kitty Wells, Pearl Butler, Connie Smith and Minnie Pearl, were also in that film. My sister Marsha was a hair-dresser back then and she did Dottie's hair and for most of the girls in that movie. She even got hair-styling credits.

After Dottie had attained a great deal of success and her marriage failed, her time spent with me became limited, which is what happens when your time is suddenly not your own. Being in the business, I understood this. Demands are being made from everyone and they're coming from all directions. It's hard on an artist because they don't want it that way, but it's what happens when you become successful.

There were times, however, that she and I would plan a special day where we could get away from the phones and just talk and visit and renew our friendship. We had planned one of those special days the last time we talked, but it was just not to be.

I remember Dottie and Bill were to go out of town the day I went into labor with my daughter Joy, but they came to the hospital and stayed until she was born. The last four hours of my labor, Dottie held my hand and later told me that she had all four of her kids again watching me try to have mine!

Joy was born on April 7. Bill's birthday is April 11. I went into labor on the 6th and after a long drawn-out affair, she was born at 12:55 a.m. on the 7th. For some reason, Bill thought if I held off having her until after midnight, she'd be born on his birthday. Well, it was after midnight and they told me that everyone was congratulating him until Dottie said, "Bill, what is the matter with you; this is the 7th and your birthday isn't until the 11th." They said then he began yelling for me to hold off four more days!

There were several others waiting for Joy to be born. There again Charlie Dick comes into the picture. He was there along with Mary Reeves, Wilma Burgess, Ginny King (Ginny and I worked together at Jim Reeves Enterprises), and my sisters Glenda and Marsha. From what they all told me they had a regular party and I believe the hospital staff threatened to make them leave. Reportedly, Mary Reeves put a daffodil in her teeth and danced down the hall! All stayed until Joy was born, except Charlie who stayed until I was moved to a room and waited until they brought Joy to me for the first time.

While Dottie was living in East Nashville, I worked some for her helping answer mail. When I left Jim Reeves Enterprises (when Mary allowed her husband Terry to let both Darla Kent Dorris and I go), Dottie was the first to call and offer a job. She had an office in her home in Franklin, Tenn., by then and I thought it was too far from where I lived to commute. I've regretted that I didn't accept her offer many times.

When Joy was about 2 years old, Dottie gave her a registered Wheaten — soft-whitish Scottie dog, named Melody. We loved her so much and kept her for nine years. That was just one of many thing Dottie gave us, but best of all was her friendship.

In September 1991, when I went to the funeral home to pay my final respects, Morris (Moe), Dottie's eldest son, told me I was the first friend of his Mom's that he could remember visiting their home. It gave me a warm, yet sad feeling to hear this.

Dottie, all the things we shared will always be just a sweet memory away, and those so-called friends who betrayed your trust won't really gain a thing. If the truth was known, I'll bet they've regretted what they did and realize that they made a big mistake, but like them, their names are unimportant. They know who they are, but I'm glad you shared who they were with me.

I spent some time with your kids when you were in the hospital (and also met Kenny Rogers, who had come by to visit) and it was hard, because I knew what they were going through. I hurt for each of them, and I couldn't believe how grown-up they all were. I'm proud of each of them, as I know you were. Shelly is so pretty, sweet and talented, and Kerry has a wonderful faith that he is sharing. Moe is strong and solid and Dale is kind and gentle. They each are a part of you. They miss you as a Mom, I along with many others will miss you as a friend, and the world misses Dottie West. (Dottie went home to be with the Lord, Sept. 4, 1991, at age 58.)

Joyce and Dottie.

Dottie all dolled up.

Bing Crosby and Bob Hope, 'Road' movie pals.
Bing dug cowboy songs, notably Cindy Walker's.

BOB HOPE...

I was on my way to Madison, Fla., to visit a friend, William E. (Bubba) Greene, back in the early 1970's. Of course, I had to change planes in Atlanta. It seems anywhere you go in the South, you have to change planes in Atlanta!

While waiting on my plane, I decided to give my friend Betty (B.Z.) Jacobs a call, as I had some time to kill. I first met B.Z. in 1958, when she came to Nashville with Patsy and Charlie Dick, and we came to be good friends. She has since died. While talking with her on the phone, I looked up and who should be walking up the concourse but Bob Hope, carrying an umbrella!

I couldn't believe it, as no one was with him, and no one bothered him. I told B.Z. who was walking toward me, and she couldn't believe it either! When he got even with me, he stopped. I suppose he stopped because I had stopped talking on the phone and stood there staring at him! He said hello, and asked how I was doing. I do not remember what I said or if I said anything. I was stunned that he had spoken to me, even though I was still on the phone.

This is one memory that has always meant so much over the years. Just thinking about it today makes me smile. Imagine the renowned Bob Hope stopping to say hello to a stranger, and to ask how I was? I'm so glad that I have had it to share in this book. Others have enjoyed hearing about it, when I've related it to them. I hope you will smile a little, too, as you read this. Mr. Hope, thank you for taking time to be so nice. You will never know what that brief moment has meant to me. You did not have to say hello to me, and I certainly wouldn't have thought anything of it, had you not. But from that moment on, I knew you were the special person that you always appeared to be. Incidentally, Bob introduced two classic songs to movie audiences, "Thanks For the Memory" and "Buttons and Bows." Thanks for *my* memory, Bob. (He died on July 27, 2003, at age 100.)

MARLON BRANDO...

In 1968, Mary Reeves took her staff to New York to watch Jim Reeves' band The Blue Boys perform at the Nashville Room in the Taft Hotel. The entire entourage decided to have dinner in the Tiki Room, a Polynesian restaurant. While eating, a small commotion within the restaurant occurred and we were told that movie star Marlon Brando had entered and gone into a private dining area.

I told Darla Kent Dorris that this would be a good time for us to go to the powder room. We did so on purpose, as I wanted to see what the commotion was all about and if he really was dining there. On our way back to our table, we passed the dining room where Marlon was seated and he had already been served. He was alone. I told Darla I just had to go introduce myself or say hello or something! She really didn't want to, but finally agreed to go with me anyway.

I will never ever forget it! I mean I'm a big fan (I sat through "Sayonara" seven times before leaving the theater), and this is one of my all-time favorite actors that I'm about to meet - and he's five feet from me! Now by this time, my conscience starts to bother me a little. I'd been in Music City for over 10 years and I knew better, but I just couldn't help it. I had to do this even knowing that one thing an entertainer hates is to have his or her meal interrupted.

I braved it anyway and eased over to his table knowing this was it, no doubt the only time in my life I'd ever have an opportunity to see, much less speak to Marlon Brando ever again. I had heard all about how he was hard to get along with, and that he wasn't very nice to his public, so the first thing I did was apologize for interrupting his dinner, explaining I just had to say hello and let him know what a huge fan I was. I introduced myself and Darla to him. He was so very gracious. He said he didn't mind that we had interrupted his meal and asked us why we were in New York and chatted in general with us for a while. I think we answered him, but I would not swear to anything.

I do remember apologizing once again for barging in on his privacy, but as I left him, I took this wonderful visit and filed it away in my memory to be remembered time and time again. If you have ever been a fan of someone and finally meet that person, then you know what I was feeling. It was wonderful! What a high!

Mr. Brando, no matter what has been written against you, my memory only sees a kind, gracious, caring , gentleman . . . I'm still a fan. (Marlon Brando died July 1, 2004, at age 80, of lung cancer.)

MAE BOREN AXTON ...

When I decided to do this book, I made a list of most of the ones that I wanted to write about. I have tried to write about Mae Axton, but I keep stopping and going on to another instead. How can I put into words just how I felt about this lady, this friend, this legend of the music business. She did so much for so many and still found time to be a friend of mine.

I first met Mae when working for Jim Reeves, and she was in town during one of the DJ Conventions (Mae said it was the convention of 1958). I would never dispute her, that's for sure, so guess that's when it was. Jim was killed in 1964, and it was long before that. I just know that I knew her for more than 30 years, and who's counting.

Through Mae, I have met some pretty interesting and very nice people, such as actors Ken Kercheval and Denver Pyle and their wives, singer Marie Osmond and of course, Mae's son, Hoyt Axton. Those are just a few names that come to mind. Before I stop writing about her, I'm sure there will be others I'll remember.

Mae has written many songs and has had them recorded, but I suppose the one that everyone will remember the most is "Heartbreak Hotel," which she co-wrote with Tommy Durden. This song was Elvis Presley's very first million seller (and now a Grammy Hall of Fame Record). She knew Elvis quite well and helped to guide him in the early years of his illustrious career. She did this for many artists, such as Johnny Tillotson, Reba McEntire, and Willie Nelson, to name just a few.

In 1975, Mae introduced Bill Rains of Billings, Mont., to Mary Reeves and her staff at Jim Reeves Enterprises. And since I was a part of her staff, I met him also. Bill and all of his family and I have shared a wonderful friendship ever since, all due to this wonderful lady, Mae Axton.

Bill is quite well-known not only in Billings, but worldwide as he is a wonderful sculptor of bronze figures, as well as a terrific artist of paintings in both oils and watercolors. Jim Reeves was the very first artist that he did a bronze sculpture of, but it was only 30 inches high. He later did *bigger than life* sculptures of other artists, but I will go into that in his segment.

When he did a three-phased bronze sculpture of Elvis, depicting the three time eras of his life, which he titled "Journey to Graceland," Mae was along, as was I, for the unveiling of the bronze in Memphis, Tenn., which took place on Elvis' birthday, Jan. 8, 1986. Prior to the Memphis unveiling, Mae kept it at her home in Hendersonville, and many came to view it while it was still in the Nashville area. She even gave a reception for Bill, so he could show his work to the media and others in the music and related industries. Mae was like that. She was always there to lend that helping hand whenever it was needed. In fact, in my opinion, so much of the time she over-extended herself with her helpfulness and her graciousness. Because she was this kind of person, at times I feel she was taken advantage of. However, I also know that she was happier when she was doing for someone else, and it was very hard for her to say no, when she felt a helping hand was deserved.

Mae and I were both invited to Billings, when Bill and Melissa Rains hosted the Montana unveiling of "Journey to Graceland," and we visited the state many times after that unveiling. She and I were involved with a charity called Hands Across the Table. It was established to help out farmers that might have had a bad year, and their families, with food, clothing or even with a child's education. "Hands" was there to help wherever the need was. I helped with a celebrity auction for a couple of years, whereby I collected articles from various artists that were friends of mine. We raised quite a bit of money and I know we did help. Denny Eubank and Charlean Keller (Charlean has passed away), both of Montana, were a big part of this charity. They were introduced to us, Mae and me, by Bill Rains and because of Mae's association with Bill and my association with Mae, I have met some of the most wonderful people in the world from the "Big Sky" State. I love it there.

I know this seems to veer away from Mae from time-to-time, but it's because of her that I have been able to do so many things and meet so many people. I'll tell you that knowing her was like looking at a "who's who." She knew people from all walks of life. I believe my poem titled "Mama Mae" sums that up pretty well.

I worked with Mae for a while at DPI Records, but it did not stay in business very long. The owner was a businessman from Texas and he didn't feel like it was making him enough money, so he closed it down. However, while working with Mae from time to time, I would pick her up and take her home and one day she said she had to stop by the Union Station Hotel (one of Nashville's most beautiful hotels, and a former train station) for a few minutes, as some friends were in town and wanted to see her. Well, we waited in the lobby and who should it be but Randall Franks (Officer Randy), Alan Autry (Bubba) and David Hart (Officer Williams) of the TV show, *In The Heat of the Night,* which starred Carroll O'Connor, who wasn't along by the way. I have met Randall a few times since then and he's always so very nice - and so good-looking.

I have gone many places and done so many things with Mae that it's hard to concentrate on just what to write about, but other than the charities in Montana, we also participated in Montana's Centennial (1989) Cattle Drive. That was so much fun and I rode on a real stagecoach.

On my 50th birthday, Mae came and about stole my party from me! She gave me a gag gift that was so neat! She had filled a bag full of junk from various parts of her house. She must have cleaned out all of her junk drawers from the looks of all the items she had placed in that bag. But it really livened up the party. Everyone got such a kick out of her.

For Doyle Wilburn's funeral, Mae wrote the eulogy. She called it *Doyle's Coronation.* It was beautifully written, as only Mae could have done it. Mae was known to about everyone in the music Industry as "Mama Mae" and it's a title that fit her perfectly, as she was like a mama to so many in and out of the music scene.

She was always ready to help the underdog. Like in my poem, if you didn't have the opportunity to meet her, then you have truly missed a blessing and Mae, I wish I could thank you for all the good times and all the many introductions to those that I would never have had the opportunity to meet, had we not been friends.

Another one that I met was Dennis Weaver and his wife, Jodie. I first met Dennis when he was going to record with Ray Pennington as his producer. Ray worked for Mary in our publishing companies at that time, and he asked me if I would go to the airport to pick him and his son up. Joy and I did just that, I remember that night so well.

While we were in the baggage area waiting for Dennis' luggage, Jimmy Dean came by where we were waiting and walked up to Joy, my cute little daughter, who was about 12 years old and said, "Hi, I'm Jimmy Dean." Joy grew up around all the artists and was not impressed and answered him with "I know who you are." She almost sounded nasty. He didn't say any more and walked away.

I got to know Dennis and Jodie better when they would visit Mae at her home. I met him on several occasions there. He died from cancer on Feb.24, 2006, at age 81, and was probably best known for his roles in the TV series *Gunsmoke* (as Chester) and *McCloud.*

Mae, if you happen to be looking down from your home on high, I just want you to know that my life has been made so much richer from having known you. You knew I loved you, but now I want the world to know that I truly did love you.

MAMA MAE
By Joyce Jackson, 1991

IN THIS INDUSTRY OF MUSIC, SHE'S A LEGEND
KNOWN TO EVERYONE AS "MAMA MAE"
IF YOU HAVEN'T HAD THE PRIVILEGE TO KNOW HER
YOU'VE TRULY MISSED A BLESSING ALONG THE WAY

SHE WAS BORN IN THE LONE STAR STATE OF TEXAS
AND SHE IS AS PROUD OF THIS FACT AS SHE CAN BE
BUT I'LL BET IF YOU ASKED HER TODAY WHERE HOME IS
SHE'D JUST AS PROUDLY SAY IN TENNESSEE

MAE'S TAUGHT SCHOOL AND THE GOLDEN RULE
AND DONE A MILLION AND ONE OTHER THINGS
SHE'S WRITTEN POEMS AND SHE'S WRITTEN SONGS
AND WROTE THE FIRST MILLION SELLER FOR THE KING

BUT ELVIS WAS JUST ONE OF MANY
YOUNG ARTISTS SHE'S HELPED ON THEIR WAY
IN REACHING THEIR GOALS AND BECOMING KNOWN
MOST OF THE TIME DONE WITH LOVE, NOT PAY

THERE WAS ELVIS, ALSO REBA AND WILLIE
AND NO ONE CAN DOUBT THEIR SUCCESS
WHEN MAE WAS TOASTED HERE IN NASHVILLE
THESE TWO WERE AMONG HER SPECIAL GUESTS

IF A LIST COULD BE MADE OF THE PEOPLE SHE KNOWS
IT WOULD CERTAINLY LOOK LIKE A "WHO'S WHO"
THERE'S BEEN SINGERS, ACTORS AND SENATORS WHO ARE KIN
AND SOMEWHERE AMONG THEM SHE'D FIT ME IN, TOO

SHE WAS BLESSED WITH TWO SONS, HOYT AND JOHN
AND SHE LOVES THEM LIKE SHE LOVED NO OTHER
THE REST OF HER "KIDS" CALL HER MAMA MAE
BUT HOYT AND JOHN CALL HER MOTHER

MAE IS A MANY-SPLENDORED THING
WRAPPED UP IN LOVE WITHOUT END
SHE'S A MOTHER, SHE'S A WOMAN, SHE'S A LADY
AND BEST OF ALL, MAMA MAE'S MY FRIEND

Mae Axton was truly my friend. I met her in October after moving to Nashville in January 1958. I also worked for Mae at DPI Records and I kept her books for her several years. I knew her like no one else did, the behind-the-scenes Mae, the Mae that wasn't on display, the heart of Mae. I loved her so much; she was like a second Mom and I also know she loved me.

Mama Mae Axton, if I could have one wish, this is what it would be: I'd like to be the kind of friend that you have been to me. I love and miss you so much. Mae went to her home on high, April 9, 1997.

Mae and Joyce at a birthday bash for George Jones,
with singer T. Graham Brown and Tammy Wells.

DOYLE'S CORONATION DAY
By Mae Boren Axton

I looked at the face in the casket
And I saw God's healing hands
He had touched Doyle's soul and called him home
God's son . . . A friend . . . A loving man.

And a message was left through the whimsical smile
And I could hear Doyle start to sing
"Oh grave, where is thy victory?"
"Oh death, where is thy sting?"

And I knew death was but a passing
From man's vision into God's.
And Doyle had gone to glory
With the Christian's Staff and Rod.

So Bugler, sound the victory song
"Doyle's Coronation Day"
And let us always feel the love
He gave along the way!

"He is not dead," I heard the words
And I knew the words were true.
He was only tired and needed rest
In a home with a better view.

I know that he is in that home,
And there's peace and beauty there.
God's richest treasures find sweet rest
In a golden room upstairs.

Our hearts are lonely through the day
We want him with us here.
But then we know he'll welcome us
When we can come upstairs.

So sing on sweet singer, sing your song
We'll hear them through the years.
And we all will share the memories
Of joys you gave while you were here.

Sing on Sweet Singer, Sing on!

OPRAH WINFREY ...

As many already know, Oprah is from Nashville, She wasn't born there, but grew up there and got her start in television there. She was on Channel 5 and subsequently did the weather and co-anchored the news, as well. I did not know her and still don't, but she once did a good deed for us.

When Joy was in grade school, the school didn't have air-conditioners. We, the PTA members, held carnivals each year to raise money to put air-conditioners in the school. The school board told us there was not enough money allotted, but if we raised enough money to have them installed, they would see they were maintained.

It was in the early 1970's when we decided to have a talent contest among the children in school, which only went to the sixth grade. Of course, we needed judges and since I worked in the music business, they felt I could obtain the judges, so I was assigned that task. Oprah was the first one I called, as she was a familiar face on local TV. I also asked one of her co-workers, Harry Chapman, who recently retired. They both said they would be happy to do this. I then asked Rudy Kalis, who did the sports for Channel 4 and he also agreed. Those were the only three I asked. I doubt very seriously if Oprah even remembers coming to Chadwell School to help judge our little talent contest, but the important thing is that I remember and I'm not the only one who does.

Oprah worked hard to climb the ladder of success and with success comes criticism. Even though I don't always agree with you or your topics, I'm still proud of the fact that you were there for us Oprah, when we needed you and you deserve the success that you have gained, as I know at times it hasn't been easy, but you have the staying power, and for that I applaud you.

Whenever someone has put you down, I have always related my story about your being our judge and how you freely gave of your time, and it always made a difference in how they were feeling about you. I know our association was brief, but I am truly thankful that God allowed our paths to cross one time, and I do wish you continued success in your endeavors.

Watching Willie

Country music star Willie Nelson relaxes in a golf cart he used while playing golf at the Heritage Country Club near La Grange last Friday. Willie and his band performed at the Kentucky State Fair Saturday night. [Photo by Lisa Kitchen]

WILLIE NELSON ...

It was around 1960, when I first met Willie Nelson. Hank Cochran introduced us. Willie was then married to his first wife, Martha (Matthews, whom he met as a Cherokee waitress) and Hank was very high on Willie's songwriting.

I really didn't get to know him personally, but I would see him around town and he always spoke, but was a very quiet person. He still is as a matter of fact. I really liked his style of singing and still have some of his old Liberty singles. Back then, no one but the people in the music business seemed to enjoy Willie. I was a fan even then and still am today.

After Willie had worked with various artists while living in Nashville (Ray Price and Faron Young are two I remember he worked with), he moved to Houston, Texas. He was living in Houston and had come back to Nashville to visit. At any rate, Roger Miller, Willie, myself and several others were up in WSM's Studio A in the old National Life Building where Ralph Emery did his all-night radio show (I used to go to that broadcast a lot back then). This was around late 1962. I know it was before Patsy Cline was killed (March 5, 1963). Roger had to leave and he and Willie were talking about Roger's upcoming Houston date and they planned to get together. Willie failed to get Roger's phone number. I had it because Barbara (Roger's wife at the time) and I were pretty good friends. So I gave it to him, knowing Roger wouldn't mind.

About two weeks after being at Ralph's show, my phone rang at midnight. I'm half asleep and answer the phone as this voice on the other end says, "Hi Joyce, this is Willie Nelson." I remember I dropped the phone, then grabbed it back, thinking I'm having a dream, but if I'm not let me say something so he won't hang up. I think I said hi or hello or something like that. I couldn't believe it was really Willie calling. He had lost Roger's number and had called Hank Cochran to see if he had it, and Hank told him no, then Willie told Hank that I had it. Hank said he had my number and Willie could call me. So Hank gave Willie my number and that's why he called, and I'm sure glad I was home. What a thrill to be called by Willie, even though it was midnight!

I got to know Willie a little better after he married Connie (Koepke, wife #3). He had started recording for RCA, and Felton Jarvis was his producer. Felton was also Elvis Presley's producer. This was during the time when I had the promotion department in the RCA Building. I also got to know Connie pretty well. I would go to Willie's session and she and I would talk while he was recording. Once she invited me over to their hotel room after the session and we visited for quite some time. They had both their little girls by then, but they were very little. In fact, the youngest was still in diapers.

Despite two early Top 10's (the first "Willingly" in 1962, with second wife Shirley Collie), Willie still hadn't "made it" as a name artist, but his songwriting was tremendous. By then, he'd had "Hello Walls" by Faron Young, "Crazy" by Patsy Cline and :"Funny How Time Slips Away" by pop artist Jimmy Elledge and country's Billy Walker. "On The Road Again," which he wrote, was a biggie for him, as was "Always On My Mind." That one wasn't written by him, but by Wayne Carson, Johnny Christopher and Mark James. And, or course, who could ever forget Fred Rose's "Blue Eyes Cryin' In the Rain," which was the song I feel that made him an artist, and not just a songwriter. Willie won a Grammy for both "On The Road Again" and "Always On My Mind," but one of my very favorite Willie cuts is "Angel Flying Too Close To The Ground"(which his buddy Hank Cochran also recorded on his "Make the World Go Away" album).

Anyone who knows Willie, knows that he is an avid golfer. In 1982, I had part interest in a golf and country club at LaGrange, Ky. Willie was due to play the Kentucky State Fair and the golf pro at our club and my best friend, Perla Potts Harkins, another investor in the club, called to see if I could contact Willie and extend an invitation for him to play at their club.

Willie was on the road, so I didn't' know how to contact him, but after making a few calls, found out that J.R. Cochran, Hank's son, was traveling with Willie and expected to be calling home and the agency that booked Willie, so I left word with both places to relate to J.R. why I wanted him to give me a call. J.R. did call me and I explained about the Country Club and that it wasn't far from Louisville, where they would be playing. He said he'd check with Willie and get back to me. He got back to me saying that Willie would be happy to play the club. I called my friends and they proceeded to lay out the Red Carpet for Willie and members of his band, who also wanted to play. The news clipping at the start of this section shows Willie in one of our golf carts. I saw Willie a couple of times when he was back in Nashville and he told me what a good time he had playing our club.

I worked on weekends for Frank and Jeanie Oakley for quite some time, even while I was still part of Jim Reeves Enterprises. The Oakleys were in business with Willie, maintaining the Willie Nelson And Family General Store first and later adding the Willie Nelson Museum. I helped to set up the museum and in April 1990, we opened it and I worked for them full-time that year. Willie told Frank that he would come to our Grand Opening, if we planned one. Since we were, we more or less arranged it according to Willie's schedule, as we wanted him there. Be there he was! He stayed with us some 12-plus hours and was wonderful with the people who were invited to attend the opening. He put on two shows for us, and I think he had a good time just jammin' with other artists who also attended.

My friend and writer of historical romance novels, Katherine Sutcliffe, had patterned a character in one of her books, "Renegade Love," after Willie, and asked that I get a copy to him if I could. This character was a Texas Ranger with long braids! Willie had his bus parked in back of the museum the night of the opening and occasionally he would go to the bus where he could rest and be able to talk with friends, such as Hank and other artists that he had invited on the bus. I took a copy of the book and told him Katherine's story and gave it to him. She had signed it to Willie. Later, after the IRS confiscated his personal belongings and they had been purchased by Jeanie and Frank, Jeanie found Katherine's book among these items, so he had kept it.

David McCormick, CEO of Ernest Tubb Record Shops, commissioned sculptor Bill Rains to sculpt the Ernest Tubb Humanitarian Award, given annually to a worthy someone in the music and related industries, for their outstanding helpfulness to others. The first year this was established was 1987, and Willie was the recipient. Willie was not available to attend, but his daughter Lana accepted on his behalf.

Willie had some hard trouble with the IRS, but I'm happy to say that is all behind him now and this is good, because he is just too nice a guy to have all those problems. Willie, you have always been the same to me over the years, as you were when Hank first introduced us, and I thank you for that. You have also done so much good for others over the years, giving free concerts and your involvement with Farm-Aid and the many other charitable things that you do, must be very rewarding. I'm proud to say I know you.

In 1992, Willie had leased a theater in Branson, Mo. and Jeanie and Frank Oakley set up a museum there, as well as maintaining a gift shop where Willie items were sold. They called and asked that I come over to Branson for a couple of weeks and help them out at the Ozark Theatre, and so I did. Willie was doing two shows a day almost every day, three weeks out of each month.

By this time, Willie had written a book which was an autobiography titled "Willie Nelson." I had taken a copy of his book with me, so I could get him to sign it and perhaps get a picture made with him for my book, as I did not have any even though we had been friends all those years. He and I were talking and he said that I reminded him of Patsy Bruce and that he had been trying to get in touch with her, so when I asked him to sign the book, he wrote "To Patsy, Love Willie Nelson." I thanked him and told him how much I appreciated him signing my book, but I would have liked it better had he signed it "To Joyce." He had that shocked look on his face, like he didn't know what I was talking about. I showed him what he had done and he got embarrassed and apologized several times. He said he had Patsy on his mind and without thinking, he signed it that way. He did sign another book to me and I have both books!

We had a good laugh about it and it made a good memory. While I'm on the subject of Branson, I would like to share with you just how Willie treated his fans there. He gave a solid hour-and-a-half show all of the time and most of the time it was even longer. Then he would sign autographs for over an hour after each performance. I was so impressed with how Willie treated each one who wanted an article signed. He was so kind, even though most also wanted pictures made with him. He was so sweet to the little girls who came up to the stage to give him a rose. He was also sweet to the big girls.

Thanks, Willie, for all the years of friendship, the good songs you've written, the great performances you've given and for being and staying WILLIE! As I said before, I was a fan way back then and I'm still a fan today.

WILLIE

By Joyce Jackson

IT WAS 1960, THE BEST I REMEMBER
WHEN WILLIE CAME INTO THIS TOWN
HE BROUGHT MANY SONGS AND SOME BECAME HITS
BUT AT FIRST HIS SONGS WERE TURNED DOWN

UNTIL HE MET HANK, A WRITER FOR PAMPER
WHO BELIEVED IN WILLIE AND HIS SONGS
HANK TOLD HAL HE SHOULD SIGN WILL UP
BECAUSE ALL OF WILLIE'S SONGS WERE STRONG

HAL LISTENED TO WILLIE'S SONGS THEN AGREED
TO GIVE WILLIE AND HIS SONGS A CHANCE
AND IT WASN'T LONG TILL THE SONGS YOU HEARD
WERE WILLIE'S ABOUT LOVE AND ROMANCE

THERE WAS "HELLO WALLS" BY FARON YOUNG
AND ALONG ABOUT THAT VERY SAME TIME
"CRAZY" WAS RELEASED AND TOPPED ALL THE CHARTS
AND WAS SUNG BY THE GREAT PATSY CLINE

THEN ALONG CAME "NIGHT LIFE" BY MR. RAY PRICE
THE LIST OF HITS JUST GOES ON AND ON.
AND IT'S REALLY "FUNNY HOW TIME SLIPS AWAY"
WHEN YOU'RE LISTENING TO A WILLIE NELSON SONG

WILLIE, ALL OF YOUR SONGS ARE JUST TERRIFIC
YOU'VE MADE IT BIG, YOU'RE A LEGEND, YOU'RE OK
AND I WAS A FAN OF YOURS WAY BACK THEN
WILLIE, I'M STILL A FAN OF YOURS TODAY

I THANK YOU FOR SIGNING THE BOOK YOU WROTE
BUT WILLIE, IF I'D HAD ANOTHER CHOICE
INSIDE OF YOUR SIGNING, "TO PATSY, LOVE WILLIE"
I'D PREFERRED THAT YOU'D SIGNED IT TO JOYCE

NOW THIS LITTLE JOKE BETWEEN YOU AND ME
WON'T MEAN A THING TO OTHERS WHO READ IT
BUT THE IMPORTANT THING IS THAT YOU AND I KNOW
AND THERE'S A MEMORY FOR ME WITHIN IT

SO YOU JUST KEEP WRITING AND SINGING YOUR SONGS
THE WAY THAT ONLY YOU, WILLIE, CAN DO
AND I'LL KEEP ON BEING THE FAN THAT I AM
WITH MY TREASURED MEMORIES OF YOU

I must say working with Willie was awesome!

Jody co-stars in an Annette Funicello & Frankie Avalon 'Beach' film.

JODY McCREA ...

Jody is the son of legendary screen actor Joel McCrea, who starred in many classic westerns, including "Buffalo Bill," "The Virginian" and "Ride the High Country." Back in the late 1950's, while in the Army, Jody was the spokesperson for the Armed Forces Radio & Television Services (AFRTS). The country music part of their shows were filmed in Nashville, so Jody visited *Music City* a great deal. Being secretary to Jim Reeves afforded me the opportunity to be present during much of the filming, as Jim did them quite frequently.

Jim was guest on one show that Jody emceed, *Country Style , USA,* as was Jean Shepard. They filmed several shows during the day and right; now I'm not sure if Jean was on with Jim or one of the other shows filmed that day. She and I had already become good friends by then.

Both of us started talking with Jody and for a while the three of us became pretty good friends, doing things together. In fact, Jean and Jody briefly became an item. Jean had dated Hawkshaw Hawkins for quite some time, but during this period they were having problems and were on the "outs."

Anyway, she and Jody spent as much time as they possibly could together. I got to spend some of that time with them. They would come over to my apartment and we'd go out to dinner and all-in-all, it was a lot of fun. I remember once when Jody had gone to visit his folks, Jean came over and we called Jody at home, and Joel answered the phone. It was really a big thrill for me to be able to say hello to Joel McCrea.

When Jody's stint in the Army ended, he went his way. Jean married Hawk (Hawk was killed in that plane crash that also took Patsy Cline's and Cowboy Copas' lives) and I continued working for Jim, but what fun to remember all those good times.

Jody went on to so-star in such B movies as "Beach Party," "Bikini Beach" and "Beach Blanket Bingo." A retired rancher, Jody died April 4, 2009, following a heart attack.

Dear Joyce,
    I don't know where these magazines get their information. Who am I marrying? I'm sure not anxious for that yet. To much to do. But I guess publicity is good.
    Thanks for your note + best to Mr. Reeves. Please give my love to Jean - and to Francis.
        Best always
P.S. Tom Daniel Jody hello. "Count

A postcard from friend Jody McCrea.

Sept 3 /58

Dear Joyce,
    I felt very homesick when I read your letter. I sure miss everybody I thank you for thinking of me.
    I am very excited about the record, and I hope you will like it. I will appreciate anything you can do when the record is released.
    Joyce you are a wonderful person and I hope to see you soon. Please don't forget me
        Johnny

Another postcard, this one from Johnny Tillotson.

JOHNNY TILLOTSON ...

The year was 1958 and Pet Milk, one of the sponsors of both *Friday Night Frolics* and the Saturday night *Grand Ole Opry* held a talent contest which Johnny had entered. He didn't win, but he did come in second. Margie Bowes, who later married Doyle Wilburn, won the contest and a recording contract with Hickory Records.

I have been told that it was Mae Axton who first gave Johnny directions in his music career and in fact, did bring him to Nashville for the contest. However, after coming in second, Lee Rosenberg, co-writer (with Bernard Weinman) of Elvis' million-selling hit "Too Much," took Johnny under her wing and helped him get established as an artist. It was through Lee that I met Johnny. I was there for the contest, but didn't meet Johnny until later. Lee was instrumental in helping Johnny get a contract with Cadence Records, run by Archie Bleyer, former music director for Arthur Godfrey's TV shows.

Johnny and I got to be pretty good friends back then and I have been in contact with him from time-to-time through the years. He was and still is a very special person to me. I remember one time when he was going to a show date and had to fly with a long layover in Louisville. I told him that I would have my Mom and sister Marsha go meet him, so he wouldn't have to wait alone. They did and then took him all around Louisville to help pass the time until his flight. Remember that, Johnny?

Remember, too, how we'd sneak away from Lee into the alley behind the Old National Life Building or the one behind the Ernest Tubb Record Shop? Those sneak kisses were always fun! At least they were for me. I can't help but smile a little as I write this.

Poor Lee, she just couldn't keep her eye on us all the time. Lee died several years ago. Johnny went on to become a big star with many hit recordings, but I suppose one of his biggest is the one he co-wrote with Lorene Mann titled "It Keeps Right On A-Hurtin.'" The Jacksonville, Fla., native also scored high on the pop chart with "Poetry In Motion," his breakthrough single in 1960, and his pop cover of Ernie Ashworth's "Talk Back Trembling Lips." Johnny co-starred in the 1963 teen film "Just For Fun," with Bobby Vee.

I saw Johnny again in the mid-1990's. He had come to Nashville and I was at Mae Axton's when he called her, and I got on the phone and talked with him. We decided to meet just to say hello and renew an old friendship. We did and it was wonderful seeing Johnny again.

One time Johnny wrote me a postcard saying not to forget him. I haven't. There's a copy of the postcard on the preceding page. Johnny, you remain one of my favorite memories, and I'm so glad I have it to share.

GLEN CAMPBELL ...

Long before *The Glen Campbell Goodtime Hour* TV show and even before his hit of "You've Still Got a Place in My Heart" which of course, came before "Gentle On My Mind," I was a Glen Campbell "nut."

Ralph Emery can attest to that, as I would call him almost every night and ask him to play anything by Glen. At that time, he only had two albums out, both of which I still have, even though they're now slightly worn!

When the very first Music City Pro-Celebrity Golf Tournament was established, it was played at Bluegrass Country Club in Hendersonville. Don Pierce, then president of Starday Records, was an original founder of the tournament and Mary Reeves was also involved in initially getting it established. Among the celebrities playing in that first tournament was Glen Campbell. Ralph introduced me to Glen and told him that I had to be his biggest fan, noting how I called the station all the time to play his records.

Glen Campbell takes a swing on the golf course.

I was thrilled to finally meet him. He was very nice and thanked me for all the calls to Ralph, but then he went ahead and continued playing golf. I didn't see him again until a few years later, when he came to Nashville to record. Billy Graves, an old beau of mine and still a very good friend, was working in the Nashville office of Capitol Records, and invited me to come with him and his mother to Glen's session. His mother was visiting from Delaware. Billy didn't say who was recording, but when I got there, I found out it was Glen. Wow! Another thrill!

After Glen had been recording for awhile, Billy's Mom and I decided to go outside and get some fresh air, as it was rather hot inside the old Quonset Hut. Evidently Glen was warm also because the next thing I knew, there he was saying, "Hi, I'm Glen Campbell," like I needed to know who he was! I refreshed his memory that Ralph had introduced me to him at the earlier golf tournament. He said he remembered, but I rather doubted it then, as I still do today, but that's OK. I understand that stars can't remember everything or everyone they meet. The important thing to me is that I remember.

When he got his own TV show, I never missed it. I know he was helpful in establishing many artists because of the exposure from his show. I truly feel it was Glen's show that boosted Mel Tillis' career. I'm not taking anything away from Mel or his efforts, but the network exposure surely did not hurt him any. His publishing company also aided in the success of Alan Jackson.

Glen, today I'm probably still one of your biggest fans, as I continue to enjoy your talents as singer and guitarist. You have met so many over the years and I know you don't remember any of this, but I do, and I'm so happy that our paths crossed, brief as it was, and that I have this memory to share.

JOHN D. LOUDERMILK ...

By the early 1960's, John D. Loudermilk had many hit recordings that he had written, but a few that come to mind at the moment are "Abilene," "Fort Worth, Dallas or Houston," "Break My Mind," and who could ever forget "A Rose and a Baby Ruth," all of which were recorded by his fellow North Carolinian George Hamilton, IV. (John's also a cousin to fellow artists Ira and Charlie Louvin.)

I can't remember exactly when we met, but I believe another writer that was a friend of mine, Betty Sue Perry, introduced us one night when a group of us were sitting down at Linebaugh's. A few weeks after I met John D., we were once again at Linebaugh's when he came in and joined us. I don't recall who everyone was, but I know there were seven of us in all. John was into Ghost stories and phenomenons and things of this nature, and began telling us all about this place in Chapel Hill, Tenn., where if you went at midnight on a night when it was softly raining and drove upon some railroad tracks, you would see a bright glowing light that people believed to be the ghost of a person, who had been murdered there on the tracks years ago.

Well, it just so happened that it was raining that way, so we all decided that we should go and check this ghost out! Betty Sue (she's now deceased, but was writer of the Wilburn Brothers' big hit, "Roll On, Big River" and Loretta Lynn's "Wine, Women and Song") was with us along with her sister, Bill Forshee (a photographer), John D., myself and I just can't recall who the other two were. Anyway, we all piled into John's big black Lincoln Town Car and headed out for Chapel Hill. We found the spot where we were supposed to see this glowing light. We got there a few minutes before midnight and waited and waited . . . and then waited some more; but, we never did see any light. By this time it was three in the morning before we left those railroad tracks and started back to Nashville. We had not gone very far when John began slowing down.

When we asked what was wrong, he said he had run out of gas! We thought he was kidding, because he was right in front of a motel! As it turned out, he wasn't kidding, he really had run out of gas and by now it's almost four in the morning. Some of the guys tried flagging down cars or trucks or whatever was coming down the road. I said I was going to see if I could use their telephone. That motel did not have a telephone! Not even a pay phone on the outside! We couldn't get anyone to stop and there were no phones, so there we sat!

I sat there for as long as I could, not doing anything and I told them that there were cars at the motel, so people had to be in there, and I was going to knock on doors until I aroused someone that would help us. They didn't believe that I would do that, but I did and the first door that I knocked on was an elderly couple from Duluth, Minn. I don't think they believed my story at first, but they were so nice and did come to our rescue. They took one of the guys to get some gas and brought him back and stayed there and talked with us until they were sure that the car started. We got their names and address and told them that we were all in the music business and that we'd send them some records. They wouldn't take any money for their help.

I can't say what the others did, I sent them some Jim Reeves' albums and wrote them a "thank you" letter. I got an answer back saying they were surprised to hear from me and that they hadn't believed we were who we said we were , but they said they were glad they had helped us out and thanked me for the albums. That was all I ever heard from them, but I have thought of them whenever someone mentions John D's name or I hear one of his songs. John D., I hope that you find one of these books and remember that night as I have, because it really was a night I will never ever forget! What a fun time!

HANK COCHRAN ...

I actually met Hank Cochran before he came to Nashville to live. He attended the DJ Convention here in 1959, before moving to *Music City* in January 1960. That was when I met him and I believe it was at the RCA Suite, but maybe it was on the backstairs of the old Andrew Jackson Hotel. Too many years have passed and I never thought I would need to know all the little details.

I do know that we became very good friends and we still are today, even though I'm no longer in Nashville. Hank and I have shared many things over the years. Some of these things I will share with you, and some things belong to just Hank and Me.

Not only did I become Hank's very good friend, but also his confidant and even song critic on some occasions. Many times, especially back in our earlier relationship, when-ever he would have trouble at home (which was a great deal of the time), Hank would give me a call and come over. We'd go to dinner or he'd just come by my house.

There were times that I thought Hank just argued at home with whomever he was with, so that he could then write one of his extremely good songs such as "She's Got You," "Make The World Go Away," "A Little Bitty Tear" and of course, the classic "I Fall To Pieces," which Hank co-wrote with Harlan Howard and was so beautifully sung by Patsy Cline.

Hank's first wife was named Shirley. I really liked her, but she and Hank just couldn't

seem to ever work things out so everyone could be happy. I don't really know how many times they married and divorced, but seems it was something like three times. He sure wrote a lot of great songs back then!

One night after a party, Hank got quite drunk and married a girl that he'd known for only a couple of weeks. Her name was Joyce (not me!), but Hank got that marriage annulled after he sobered up and realized what he had done. Later, he married Jeannie Seely. They stayed married for several years and during that relationship, he wrote many more hit songs including Jeannie's big hit "Don't Touch Me." It was also a big Decca record by Wilma Burgess.

Hank's wife now is Susie, but between all these marriages and all the many girlfriends, I remained his friend and even became more than that. If you were in a relationship with Hank, you had to take turns being his girlfriend. I think this is what most of them did not understand, but in many ways, I did. He was a lot of fun, so I took my turns, stayed his friend, and I have truly treasured our special relationship.

One of the first times that Hank asked me out was to go to this little place called The Corral (it has since burned down). It was in Madison and had the best steak and potato dinner for about $1.50 back then. There were also times that I would have him over to my house for dinner.

I remember when Hank got his first royalty check for "I Fall To Pieces." He bought a little farm in the rural area of Hendersonville. The best I remember it was 72 acres and I believe he paid something like $16,000 for it. He made enough to pay half of it with his first check. He was so excited about this piece of land. He called me and wanted me to go with him to see it.

I will never forget that day. He came to pick me up, it was a warm day and raining a very soft rain, more like a misty rain, and Hank and I walked the entire perimeter of that 72 acres. It was a beautiful piece of land. I remember a little rise in the backfield of the land and when you stood on it and spoke, there would be an echo. Hank stood on it and yelled, "Hank's a star." Of course, it echoes something like *"Hank's a star, star, star!"* I believe he paid the little farm off with his second check. It wasn't too long after he bought the farm that he was able to buy his first Cadillac. It was a beautiful white 1963 Cadillac, with light green upholstery. He came banging on my duplex apartment about 4 one morning, telling me to get up and go for a ride in his new car. He had been celebrating with a group of buddies and was about half high, but I got up and just put my housecoat on and went for a ride.

It was never unusual for Hank to call at any hour of the morning. Sometimes it would be for me to hear a song he'd just written or sometimes he would just be down and wanted someone to talk to. It didn't matter, our friendship grew and after I got my divorce and became a single parent, I turned to that friendship, and Hank was always there.

By the time my daughter Joy was 3 years old, Hank had gotten his second cabin cruiser which he called "The Legend." It's a good thing that boats can't talk! I really had a lot of fun during those years, and on that boat. I was still taking turns being with Hank. One night Hank called and asked me to get on the next plane and come to Atlanta. I said I would come if my sister could watch Joy. He said that he had looked Atlanta over and he couldn't find anybody worth looking at there! I laughed knowing it wasn't a big deal that he was looking, because as I said before if you wanted to be with Hank, you took turns! He'd even tell me who he was with. That was OK with me, too. It just was. I guess it was because even though I loved Hank, I wasn't "in love" with him that made the difference. I don't know or even care, I just know that he did have a ticket waiting for me at the airport and I spent a wonderful weekend with him in Atlanta.

Mel Tillis was playing The Playroom and of course, we went to his show. Before the show, Hank, Mel and I went to dinner. I don't remember the name of the place, but it was Chinese and the food was great.

At the show, we were seated at a good table up front and soon we were joined by Willie Nelson, his wife Shirley, and daughter Lana. It was really a fun evening and one filled with wonderful entertainment. Mel did a first-class show as he always does. If Hank asked you out to dinner, he always took you to the nicer restaurants.

Back then, Nashville really didn't have the variety of restaurants that they enjoy today, but I remember we were having dinner one night (Sept. 16, 1968) at St. Clair's, one of Nashville's better restaurants then, and I suppose Hank had left word with some of his friends where he would be, because he got a phone call. He came back to the table and was white as a sheet. When I asked what was wrong, he said that Roy Orbison's house was burning and someone wanted to use his boat to try to get to the house from the lake side. Roy's house was on Old Hickory Lake next to where Johnny Cash lived.

It was such a sad time for our industry, as Roy lost two sons in that fire. There were about five or six of our friends that had houseboats and yachts and sometimes we would all go out to the middle of the lake and tie all the boats together and just party all night. I remember one night that we all went to our favorite cove on Old Hickory Lake and everyone tied up together, but this time we got off the boats and built a campfire on the shore and cooked hamburgers and hot dogs. When everyone began to get sleepy, they went to their particular boat, but Hank and I got out his sleeping bag and spent the night right there beside the campfire.

Another time that stands out in my memory, was when I was to meet Leo O'Rourke, one of the friends that had a houseboat, which he kept at Old Hickory Boat Dock. He was to take me with him on the houseboat over to Anchor High Marina where Hank's boat was docked. Hank was waiting for us on his boat. When I got on Leo's boat, I found that Dallas Frazier (writer of the Oak Ridge Boys' big hit "Elvira" and Jack Greene's "There Goes My Everything") was with Leo. Dallas is one of my very favorite song-writers and my friend. I just love him. Some will remember "Alley Oop," just to name another of so many wonderful songs penned by Dallas. When we got across the lake to Hank's boat, I tried to step from one boat to the other. Hank had his hand out to reach for me, but I missed it and down I went. I had on a pantsuit that I had made and back then we were all wearing falls in our hair. My purse was in my hand and everything got soaked! Hank was so mad at both Leo and Dallas for not helping me. Actually, it was really quite funny after I dried out! When I think about that night today, it gets funnier. I had to put on Hank's robe and take those wet clothes off to dry. We hung them on various things, securing them and then ran up and down the lake drying them in the wind. What a memory!

As I reflect back, I remember that Hank was among the ones who searched for Jim when it was reported that the plane had crashed. He even went as far as contacting a medium to see if his location could be pinpointed. Jim had asked Hank to go on that business trip with him, but he'd had a previous engagement and could not go. For the biggest part of the time that I lived in Nashville, I had Hank as my friend, and Hank there is no way that I could write all the things we've shared and there have been many.

You taught me so much about life, love, sharing and caring. I value all the time we shared together. I can't help but smile when I recall some of those lessons in love and life, and I still care so much about you. You are a treasured friend, Hank, and another of the "legends" that I have written about and have been fortunate enough to call friend. Memories, boy, do we have them!

ROD BRASFIELD ...

Soon after moving to Nashville, I met Rod Brasfield. We lost this country comic that very same year, on Sept.12, 1958. He was only 48 years old.

One night while some of us were having coffee at Linebaugh's, Rod came in and joined us. I told him a joke he thought was so funny that he asked if I cared if he told it on the Opry. I told him I would be honored if he did. This happened on a Saturday night between shows, and when he went back to the Opry, he did tell that joke. I don't recall how the joke went, but the punch line was that this guy got shot with an iron bullet and may he rust in peace.

My only association with Rod Brasfield was seeing him at the Opry and sometimes down at Linebaugh's, but I always enjoyed it when he'd come in and sit with us. He always had some funny story to tell. What pleasure he and Minnie Pearl gave to so many with their Opry antics. They were such fun together.

Of course, Rod played a key role in Andy Griffith's dramatic movie "A Face In the Crowd," opposite another Kentucky-born gal Patricia Neal in 1957, and had he lived would probably have pursued additional Hollywood parts.

I still value what little time I knew him, for many have not had that pleasure or that memory; I'm glad I do. (Rod was posthumously inducted into the Country Music Hall of Fame in 1987.)

The Everly Brothers in performance.

Don, Joyce and Phil.

THE EVERLY BROTHERS ...

Don and Phil Everly were guesting on the *Grand Ole Opry,* when I met them backstage in 1957, during one of my visits. This was the year they had back-to-back #1 singles "Bye, Bye Love" and "Wake Up, Little Susie," for Archie Bleyer's independent Cadence label (also Johnny Tillotson's disc company).

Our paths did cross again after I came to Nashville to live. Don was then married to Sue (Ingraham) and they had a daughter. Some mutual friends had been invited to Don and Sue's house and they asked me to go along. I did and one thing that impressed me was a jukebox Don had in his music room. It was just like the ones that I was used to playing records on, and I couldn't believe someone could actually own one. Of course, today many people have their own jukebox as part of their décor, but then it was very rare.

It wasn't very long after my visit to Don's that I got into a conversation with Phil at Linebaugh's. It was a Friday night and as we talked somehow bowling got mentioned. We must have said we enjoyed it. At any rate, we decided to go bowling together the next day. We planned to meet at Melrose Lanes. Neither of us lived too far from there.

The next day, Phil was not the only one who came; he brought his dad Ike with him, so all of us bowled. We had such a good time and I don't know if Phil will admit it or not, but I beat both him and his Dad. Mr. Everly has since passed away, so it's Phil's word against mine.

Those were the only times that I actually spent with the Everlys, but I did get to know their Mom (Margaret) pretty well after that, but mostly through phone conversations. All of this took place a long time ago during my first years in Nashville. I hope they will remember, but if they don't, it's OK. . . I do.

Incidentally, the Brothers were inducted into the Rock & Roll Hall of Fame in 1986, and the Country Music Hall of Fame in 2001, attesting to their crossover appeal.

CINDY WALKER ...

My goodness, where do I begin with my sweet precious friend, Cindy Walker? I knew her for such a long time and loved her so much. Even when I didn't know her, I knew *who* she was, one of country music's greatest songwriters.

The first time that I saw Cindy was on TV in Louisville. She was a guest on the Pee Wee King show. So many of her songs are the standards that we are still hearing and enjoying today. Songs like "You Don't Know Me," "In The Misty Moonlight" and the songs that Jim recorded, including "Anna Marie," "A Letter to My Heart," "Rosa Rio," "This Is It" and of course the classic "Distant Drums." I don't know if it still holds true, but at one time, I believe Jim had recorded more Cindy Walker songs than any other artist. It was through Jim that I met Cindy and her mother "Mama" (Oree) Walker.

It was not only a privilege meeting these two ladies, but what an honor to have been truly blessed with having them as my personal friends for so many years. We have shared many good times together. I've cooked for them and they have for me. They have been present for the birthday parties that we had for both Mary and Jim, and were with us for some Christmas gatherings, and have spent many hours just being together and talking. Both Cindy and Mama were talkers and the stories they told would be the kind that would keep you spellbound the entire time.

Cindy has written scores for movies, been in films herself, and as a teen was a highly-acclaimed dancer performing at Billy Rose's Casa Manana in Ft. Worth, Texas.

Cindy knew everyone! She was a friend of the original Sons of the Pioneers, also Bob Wills, Tex Ritter, Roy Rogers, Gene Autry and about everyone that has ever been in the music industry and early western films. World-renowned crooner Bing Crosby recorded her song "Lone Star Trail," making it a pop Top 20 record in 1941.

Mama Oree was the daughter of Professor F. L. Eiland, an inspirational composer whose sacred songs included "Hold To God's Unchanging Hands." Is it any wonder that their stories could keep you so mesmerized? How I enjoyed listening to and absorbing all whose wonderful stories of some of the greats of our time.

One of the most outstanding attributes of both Cindy and Mama was the good they managed to see in another person. I loved this about them. We have lost both Mama Oree and Cindy now, but they were such a part of each other's lives that it's kinda good they are together again.

When I had my little girl, Joy, they sent me the most beautiful blue dress for her. I had her six-months-old picture made in it. Then a little later, Mama made a sweet little yellow dress and I had her nine-months' picture taken in it. They were always special, because they were from Mama and Cindy. I still have them today.

Cindy recorded an album of her songs that was released on Monument Records several years ago, and she told me that I would be the first she gave one to. She sent me a copy and wrote on the back, "To Joyce, this is the first one I've sent out"

Although I love most of the songs that Jim recorded over the years, I suppose that my personal favorite is "This Is It." Sometimes Jim would call Cindy and tell her that he would be recording and that he needed some material, and she would always come up with some new song for him. She was an awesome lady, and was made a charter member of the Nashville Songwriters' Hall of Fame in 1970.

When Cindy was enshrined in the Country Music Hall of Fame in 1997, she gave a luncheon for her many friends in the industry. I was invited, but was working and could not make it to the luncheon. Still she wanted me there, so I came by her hotel after I got off work and she had the chef make a special dinner just for me and we visited one- on- one. That was just the kind of person she was. See why my life has been made richer?

For the . . . Fame affair, she wore a dress that Mama had gotten her for a BMI dinner and told her that she wanted her to wear that dress when inducted into the Country Music Hall of Fame. Cindy wrote a poem about that dress and read it the night she was honored. She also made up Christmas cards with her picture wearing that dress. I received one of those special Christmas Cards, and want to share with you what she wrote to me in the card.

I talked with Cindy not long before she died and she said she wasn't feeling good, but we always managed to have a good laugh together when we talked, and did then. She was glad that I had moved to Colorado to be closer to my daughter. Mama Oree died in 1991, and Cindy joined her on March 26, 2006 (at age 87). You know that I miss you my precious friends.

THE DRESS

Cindy Walker

In the 1980's my Mother bought me a dress..For a BMI affair....And she said. "When they put you in The Hall of Fame..That's the dress..I want you to wear".. And, I said. "Oh. Mama..The Hall of Fame..Why, that will never be"..And the years went by..But my Mother's words..remained in my memory..And I know..tonight..she'd be happy..Tho she's gone now..to her rest..But I think of all..That she did for me...And, tonight..I'm wearing that dress!..

Cindy Walker

1997

Joyce and Cindy Walker.

WILMA BURGESS ...

Wilma Burgess and Ginny King moved to Nashville in 1964. Ginny started working for Jim Reeves Enterprises as our bookkeeper shortly after their move. Encouraged by no less than Eddy Arnold, Wilma began pursuing a career in country music.

Noted publisher Charlie Lamb heard her and was impressed with her unique voice and brought her to the attention of Owen Bradley, A&R director for Decca Records (Decca later became MCA Records). Owen also recorded Kitty Wells, Patsy Cline, Brenda Lee, Loretta Lynn and so many others, and was one who helped create the *Nashville Sound,* which brought so many others in the music world to our city.

Bradley liked what he heard when Wilma sang for him, and signed her to a Decca contract. Her first hit was Ray Griff's song "Baby." I used to put Joy to sleep with that recording. She also had a Top Five single with "Misty Blue" and enjoyed some success covering Hank's "Don't Touch Me," which won a Grammy for Jeannie Seely. Wilma's recording did well in both sales and airplay across the country, but Jeannie's won the awards. Their sound was different and each brought something special to their particular versions. They were both such talented singers. When Wilma's rendition of "Don't Touch Me" charted, she was booked in Ottumwa, Iowa, and Des Moines. It was on a weekend, so she wanted Ginny and I to go with her, and we did.

It was very cold and we had almost gotten to Clarksville, Tenn., when Wilma thought it would be funny to pass gas since we had the windows rolled up and being so cold, dared not roll them down. It rather backfired on her, however, because she passed a little more than gas, so we had to stop for her to rush into a restroom and change her undies. Thus we had the last laugh on her, and never did let her forget what she had tried to do to us.

Wilma was a lot of fun. Not long after the success of "Baby," "Don't Touch Me" and "Misty Blue," Wilma was in a position to buy a house and the one she bought was from Charlie Dick on Nella Drive in suburban Madison.

Wilma worked with us on many different occasions at the Jim Reeves Museum in Madison, and she also had her own club at one time called Track 9 near downtown Nashville.

When Joy turned 2 years old, Wilma and Ginny bought Joy her very first little tricycle, red and white, and Joy loved it. Wilma was unique and of a special breed, and in many ways was her own worst enemy regarding her career. But she was a kind and good-hearted woman and, I feel, extremely talented. Wilma, you were one of a kind. (She passed away Aug. 26, 2003, from a heart attack at age 64.)

Wilma and Bud Logan, duet partners, who scored on the single 'Wake Me Into Love.'

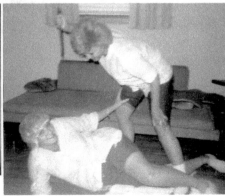

Wilma clowns around with her beautician Marsha, Joyce's sister, while having her hair done.

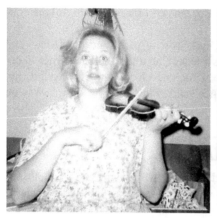

Wilma just fiddlin' around.

Wilma, manager Charlie Lamb & wife Frances.

WAYLON JENNINGS ...

The best I can remember, it was 1962 during the DJ Convention when I met Waylon Jennings for the very first time. He had just been signed to RCA, as had Dottie West. They both performed during the RCA Breakfast Show, held at that time in the old Maxwell House Hotel (that burned down in 1963). Jim Reeves emceed that particular show.

Waylon wowed everyone at the show and somehow you just knew that this man was destined for stardom. I don't think that I knew at that time that he had been a part of Buddy Holly's group, The Crickets, but, of course, it wasn't long before I did. His RCA biography included this information and the fact Waylon had given up his seat to The Big Bopper (J.P. Richardson) on the plane that crashed Feb. 3, 1959 in Iowa, taking the lives of Holly, Ritchie Valens and the Big Bopper.

Like so many others back then, Waylon had a reputation of abusing alcohol, pills and chasing women. I'm sure he did his fair share, but I really liked Waylon, the person, and felt I got to know him better when I had an office in the RCA Building. It was around 1973, when Waylon came by one day about noon. I do not know to this day why, but he did, and we sat and talked all afternoon. He had a five o'clock appointment that was only going to take about 30 minutes, he said, and asked me if I would stay there until he got back? I could tell he wanted to talk some more, so I told him that I would wait for awhile. He came back when he said he would, and we talked for another two-to-three hours.

I remember telling him that he was a big phony: That he was really a wonderful, caring person underneath this big tough front that he was wearing. He laughed and thanked me for seeing the real man underneath, but said he had to be what the people expected him to be, and that this was the key to being successful. I disagreed, and he just laughed.

Waylon is another artist that I wish I had known better. He was married and didn't travel with the same crowd that I did, but I admired him and his talent so much. More than that, I appreciate and am thankful for the opportunity of seeing *the real Waylon*. I'm proud that he always stood up for what he believed in. That's the kind of person that I met that day in my office back in 1973. I'm thankful for the wonderful memory that I now have to share.

Waylon, whose hits were many including "Brown-Eyed Handsome Man" and "Good-Hearted Woman," was married to Jessi Colter, an artist and songwriter in her own right. I loved her recording of "I'm Not Lisa," which she wrote, as well as her duets with Waylon, notably "Suspicious Minds" and "Storms Never Last." (Waylon died Feb. 13, 2002, at age 64.)

BILLY WALKER ...

When I first met Billy, he was still married to Boots, his first wife and the mother of his children. It was probably during 1959, or at the least in early 1960. We were never what you'd call really close friends, but I did get to know him pretty good, as he and his second wife Bettie both attended the same church I did.

Billy truly became a man of God, and I was deeply saddened by his untimely death on May 21, 2006. Both he and Bettie were killed in a car crash, while heading home after an Alabama show date. (Two bandmembers, Charles Lilly, Jr., and Daniel Patton, died, while their grandson Joshua Brooks was seriously injured, but did survive.)

Billy Walker, an Opry member since 1960, enjoyed hit recordings such as "Charlie's Shoes," "Cross the Brazos at Waco" and "A Million And One." He was a super nice man and I'm very thankful I knew him. His and Bettie's passing truly left a void in the music industry in Nashville.

HANK THOMPSON ...

Hank Thompson and I met a couple of times, and for that I am most thankful. The first time was again during a DJ Convention, this one at the Ramada Inn in Nashville. Charlie Dick and I went to his room, as there was a jam session going on.

That was a great deal of fun, and then the other time we met was at a Texas Day, conducted in liaison with the Jim Reeves Museum in 1982. I felt that he didn't remember me from the Convention, but he said he did, as he came over to me and began a good conversation.

I really enjoyed his style of country music, having been a huge fan ever since "The Wild Side of Life" and "The New Green Light" came out by him. Incidentally, his #1 "The Wild Side of Life," the top song of 1952, inspired my friend Kitty Wells' answer song "It Wasn't God Who Made Honky Tonk Angels," which launched her legendary career (after 15 years as an entertainer on radio).

Hank was finally inducted into the

Country Music Hall of Fame in 1989. After suffering from lung cancer, he died on Nov. 6, 2007, at age 82. He's truly missed by all in the industry, as well as his many fans.

BILLY GRAMMER ...

I believe I came to Nashville before Billy and his wife Ruth did, but actually we came pretty close to the same time, and I have known them many years, and you won't meet two nicer people. I love them both very much.

Ruth, Mary Reeves and I used to go out together quite a bit back in the early 1960's and we bowled together a lot. I wasn't in the same league that Ruth and Mary were, but we did spend a lot of time at the bowling alley. I have been to Billy and Ruth's house on many occasions and when they had their 50th wedding anniversary, I was invited to attend the celebration at the Grand Ole Opry House. Their daughter Donna called and invited me, and I wrote a poem for them. This is the poem:

BILLY AND RUTH . . .

HOW LONG HAS IT BEEN, I JUST CAN'T REMEMBER
SEEMS LIKE I'VE ALWAYS KNOWN BILLY AND RUTH
WHERE DID THE YEARS GO, HOW MANY DECEMBERS
I CAN'T TELL YOU THAT, BUT THIS IS THE TRUTH

A SWEETER COUPLE YOU WILL NEVER FIND
THOUGH TO THEM TRIALS AND TROUBLES HAVE COME
I'VE NEVER SEEN THEM TREAT ANYONE UNKIND
THEY'RE GOOD PEOPLE AND THEY ARE SO MUCH FUN

IN THE EARLY YEARS, RUTH WAS A BOWLER
AND SHE PLAYED THAT GAME OH SO WELL
RUTH AND MARY REEVES WERE ON THE SAME TEAM
THEY WERE SERIOUS ABOUT THE GAME, YOU COULD TELL

SHE LIKES TO HAVE FUN AND GO OUT ON THE TOWN
WHICH WE DID QUITE OFTEN BACK THEN
THE "WE" BEING RUTH, MARY REEVES AND ME
AND MAYBE A FEW OTHER GOOD FRIENDS.

BILLY PLAYED THE OPRY AND SANG HIS SONGS
AND HE WORKED THE ROAD BACK THEN, TOO
WE ALL REMEMBER "I'VE GOTTA TRAVEL ON"
BUT THIS WAS JUST ONE OF THE SONGS HE WOULD DO

THEY RAISED A FAMILY OF TWO GIRLS AND A BOY
AND I KNOW THEY ARE PROUD OF EACH ONE
WHEN IT COMES TO BEING GRANDPARENTS
THEY BOAST OF THEIR GRANDKIDS, AS WE ALL HAVE DONE

NOW FOR THOSE THAT ARE WONDERING HOW I HAVE FIT IN
TO THIS LIFE OF RUTH'S AND BILL'S
REALLY IT'S QUITE SIMPLE, I'M SIMPLY THEIR FRIEND
I LOVED THEM WHEN WE MET AND I LOVE THEM STILL

SO CONGRATULATIONS BILLY AND RUTH
FOR FIFTY GOLDEN YEARS WELL DONE
MAY GOD BLESS AND KEEP YOU IN HIS WONDROUS LOVE
LIKE THE LOVE THAT HE HAD FOR HIS PRECIOUS SON

I LOVE YOU SO MUCH
By Joyce Jackson, Oct. 29, 1994

Ruth along with my sister Marsha, my Mom and Rita, Ruth's niece, were among the ones who helped in the search for Jim when his plane went down. Billy has enjoyed many facets of the music industry. He is a great guitarist and at one time even had a guitar named after him. He joined the Opry in 1959, after having a big crossover hit recording that year of "I've Gotta Travel On." He was inducted into the Illinois Country Music Hall of Fame in 1969. Now retired, he lives in Southern Illinois, but what a pleasure it has been knowing them both. I would not have traded that for anything. The Grammers are so loved.

THE GLASER BROTHERS ...

These guys were like brothers to me. Maybe not so much Tompall, but Chuck and Jim were. They moved to Nashville in 1958, shortly after I did, and toured with Marty Robbins for many years. I believe their first recording contract was for Robbins Records, Marty's label.

Jim dated and later married one of my roommates, Mary Jane Evans. For a little while, Chuck dated my sister Glenda; however, his heart belonged to a girl back in

Nebraska, and he later married Bev. We all became such good friends, and Jim and Chuck were at our apartment quite a bit. We are still friends.

They had some of the best harmony that anyone could have and later each did some solo recordings, but in my opinion Jim had the best solo voice of the three and had some wonderful recordings, including "You're Gettin' To Me Again," a #1 single. What a voice! I suppose the biggest hit they had as a group was a song titled "Lovin' Her Was Easier (Than Anything I'll Ever Do Again)," written by Kris Kristofferson. Tompall was part of the "Outlaw Movement," that included Waylon Jennings and Willie Nelson, and performs on the historic RCA album, "The Outlaws," which went double platinum in 1976.

When my sisters, Glenda and Marsha, and my friend Barbara Byrd, had a going away party for me, when I moved to Colorado, Jim, Jane, Chuck and Bev were all there to say their goodbyes and offer well wishes for me. How I loved all the years that we've known each other and the good times we've shared. All of you are so special to me. Have I been blessed or what?

JIMMY C. NEWMAN ...

Since Jimmy and his wife Mae were good friends of Mary and Jim's, I met them through the Reeves, and was around them a great deal.

Jimmy is such a rare talent, hailing from Louisiana and a true Cajun *aye eee!* Whenever we had parties at Jim and Mary's house or at the office, Jimmy and Mae were always invited and most of he time, were able to come. Jimmy should always wear a white hat 'cause he is truly a good guy and has always been so nice to me.

Mae and Jimmy both know how to cook that delicious, spicy Cajun food and I have had the pleasure of sampling some of it. *Yum! Yum!*

We had a get-together back in 1967, and Mae brought cut-up veggies and a curry sauce which I just fell in love with. She gave me the recipe and I have made it many, many times over the years and always credit her for it. It is excellent on raw veggies. I would write it down here, but I'm afraid Mae would not want me to, so get it from her!

Jimmy has enjoyed a most successful career with hits like "Cry, Cry Darling" and "A Fallen Star," and he has been a part of the *Grand Ole Opry* since 1956. Love you both and am so happy we met, and that we've shared so many years as friends

Jimmy C. and wife Mae.

Jean Shepard, Jimmy C. and Joyce.   *Newman again with Joyce Jackson.*

BOBBY BARE ...

Bobby Bare is one I have known for many years and have been around a great deal, though we never really did a lot of things together. I did take acting classes with his wife Jeannie, and we had a lot of fun doing that. I would run into Bobby at many of the various functions that went on in Nashville and he was always the same Bobby every time we met.

I remember that he and Jeannie came to our special opening for The Jim Reeves Museum in 1981, and Bobby wanted to know how I managed to get the street that ran by the museum named after me. It was at the corner of Gallatin Road and Joyce Lane. They have since torn it down and put up a Home Depot, and that is one thing that I will never understand because The Jim Reeves Museum was housed in The Evergreen Place, which Mary Reeves purchased in 1980, and was built during George Washington's second term of office (1794) and listed on the U.S. Historical Register.

Anyway, I told Bobby that I was special and that's why they named the street after me. Of course, it was named that long before I ever came to Nashville, but it did make for a good conversation piece with different ones a lot of times.

Bobby and my daughter Joy share the same birthday, April 7th. I suppose Bobby will best be remembered for his big hits "All-American Boy" and "Detroit City." The first came out in 1958 under the name of Bill Parsons, though it was really Bobby, who was then in the Army, performing. It went to #2 in the *Billboard* pop charts. "Detroit City" earned a Grammy as Best Country Single in 1963.

Jim cut one of Bobby's songs that was in an album called "Teardrops On the Rocks," but one of my favorite Bobby Bare songs was "Marie Laveau," his first record to go #1 (in 1979). One of the best things that I love about Bobby is that he is truly a super nice guy and a little shy. I am happy that I got to know you Bobby, even if we didn't run in the same circle.

JACK GREENE ...

It seems like Jack Greene first went to work for Ernest Tubb somewhere around 1961, and that's when I met him. He was Tubb's drummer in the Texas Troubadours band as well as special artist on his touring show. Later, he branched out on his own and had many hit recordings, but I suppose he is most remembered for his huge hits "There Goes My Everything," written by my friend Dallas Frazier, "All The Time" written by Mel Tillis and Wayne Walker, and "Statue of a Fool" by Jan Crutchfield.

Jack was another artist that came to Billings for Hands Across the Table, and always put on a top-notch show. He also attended the same church on many occasions that I did. We didn't really do things together, but he was always so pleasant whenever we did happen to be at the same place, and never failed to ask how Joy was. When I was back in Nashville a few years ago, I went to a ROPE meeting and Jack was there and even though he wasn't in the best of health, performed, and did so beautifully. He signed a photo to me "To One of a Kind," but to me Jack is the "One of a Kind." Love ya, Jack, and thanks for so many years of good songs and good memories.

Jack and the author's daughter Joy.   *Jack and Joy again, with Joyce.*

GOLDIE HILL & CARL SMITH ...

I have been a fan of both Carl and Goldie's for about as long as I can remember. I know when I first saw them it was prior to my high school days and I was so thrilled to finally get to know them. I still have several 78rpm recordings by Carl and one of my fondest memories was going to their house for dinner with Margie Perkins Beaver. (Margie was once married to the late Luther Perkins, guitar player for Johnny Cash, and tragically lost his life in a house fire.) I do not remember what all Goldie had prepared,

but the main thing that I wanted was macaroni and tomatoes. My Mom used to fix that dish and Goldie prepared it just like Mom's. Another time I took Joy with me, and she and their children played together quite a bit. I remember they had this big dog they called "Blue."

Carl had many hits back in the 1950's such as "Hey, Joe," "Loose Talk" and one of my very favorites "Mr. Moon." Goldie had a hit duet with Justin Tubb called "Lookin' Back to See" and the #1 answer to Slim Willet's song, "Don't Let the Stars Get in Your Eyes," called "I Let the Stars Get in My Eyes." Goldie is Tommy Hill's sister and Tommy was one of Jim's earlier band members.

Although I was not around either of these fantastic people much, I do value what time I spent with them. Both Tommy and Goldie are gone now. Carl was inducted into the Country Music hall of Fame finally in 2003.

A 1950s' Goldie Hill with Joyce.   *Goldie's brother Tommy Hill.*

BILL MONROE ...

Bill Monroe was known as The Father of Bluegrass, a form of music he's credited with helping to invent. We saw one another on many occasions, either at the Opry or one of many Nashville music functions.

When Bill decided to open a Bill Monroe Bluegrass Museum, I was asked to make the cake for the Grand Opening. What a cake it was! It was a sheet cake 36" X 54" in size. I had to cover a 4' X 4' piece of plywood to put it on. (See accompanying photo). My sister Marsha and brother-in-law Stu Basore came to the house to help me load it into the back of my station-wagon (the same one that took "Journey to Graceland" to Memphis). We had to hold it at an angle to get it out my back door, but we made it and the cake was a big hit at the opening.

Bill, of course, was also an accomplished songwriter with such standards as "Blue Moon of Kentucky," an early cut by Elvis Presley, and "Uncle Pen" (revived by Ricky Skaggs, who took it to #1). Bill was elected to the Country Music Hall of Fame in 1970, and made a charter member that year in the Nashville Songwriters' Hall of Fame, and won a Grammy Lifetime Achievement Award in 1993. Bill Monroe died Sept.9, 1996, at age 84, following a stroke.

JOHNNY RUSSELL ...

Johnny said that it was 1959, when we first met and Jim introduced us. I couldn't remember the exact year, but he did and he remembered where it was. I had also forgotten that! Thank goodness he remembered and verified the time and place. It was in the old National Life Building's artists lounge, which was really a foyer for the men's room. I think there was a cabinet with slots separating the various artists' mail and there was one kind of couch or settee facing each other as you came in.

Johnny had written this song that was to become the flip side of Jim's million-selling "He'll Have to Go" titled "In A Mansion Stands My Love." Jim knew that he wanted to record this song and asked me if I would tell Johnny that he wanted to talk with him. I did and they talked. I didn't know until a later conversation with Johnny that he had talked with Chet Atkins about his song before talking to Jim. Chet told Johnny that Jim wanted to record it, but that Jim would ask Johnny for half writer's credit on it and Chet told Johnny not to give it to him. Sure enough, that is what Jim wanted to talk to Johnny about. He asked, Johnny refused, and Jim recorded the song anyway. He and Johnny became very good friends and I know that Jim went to bat in Johnny's behalf on some other things that Johnny had written which had been published by another company and they were trying to get out of paying Johnny his writer's royalties.

Johnny and I became friends even though Johnny wasn't making his home permanently in Nashville at that time. He was living in Fresno, Calif., and was a disc jockey, but would come to Nashville from tim-to-time to try and get his songs recorded. I remember he was here for the 1960 DJ Convention. This was after Jim's record had sold a million copies, and of course, that meant that Johnny's side also sold a million copies. Joe and Audrey Allison are the writers of "He'll Have to Go" and Joe always got involved in the activities of the convention. Back then everyone went to all the events. They were a lot of fun then. Joe told me this story; however, I did witness part of it myself. Joe did not know who Johnny was, but Johnny knew who Joe was and that he wrote "He'll Have to Go." Everywhere Joe went during this particular convention, Johnny followed him. Joe said that everywhere he turned there was this little fat boy right behind him and whenever he'd turn to look at Johnny, all Johnny would do was smile at him and say "thank ya." This went on for a couple of days or so, and Joe said it finally got the best of him, so he confronted Johnny saying, "What is it you want, you have followed me around for two solid days and all you ever do is smile and say 'thank ya.'" Joe said Johnny just looked at him, smiled and said, "I wrote the flip side of 'He'll Have to Go,' thank ya." I hope when this is read that it's as funny as it was to Joe and me and others that knew both of them.

When Johnny did move to Nashville, he moved in with Vic McAlpin and Archie Campbell. You talk about a threesome! That house must have been a riot all the time. I felt lucky to have known both Vic and Archie. I worked with Vic, as he was a writer for Jim Reeves' Acclaim publishing company, and Archie had an office down the hall from us in the RCA Building. It was then that Johnny got his contract with RCA as an artist. He had already enjoyed a great deal of success as a writer with not only the one by Jim, but he also wrote the big hit by Buck Owens titled "Act Naturally" and another of my very favorite songs, "Making Plans," The Wilburn Brothers had a success on that one, as did Porter Wagoner and Dolly Parton. Johnny became successful as an artist with hits such as "Catfish John" and "Rednecks, White Socks and Blue Ribbon Beer." He said that his one big dream was to be a member of the *Grand Ole Opry* and he also made that a reality in 1985.

He once told me that he just couldn't believe that he had been able to do and be everything that he ever wanted. He was a successful songwriter, a successful artist, and a member of the Opry. I personally feel that he obtained his real happiness when he found a church where he could grow in the Lord. That church was the same one that I finally found, and we enjoyed an even better friendship there. I value and treasure all the years of friendship and fellowship that Johnny and I shared, both in music and at church. He was one of Nashville's truly fine people and it's a joy for me to share my friend with you. Johnny died July 2, 2001, at age 61.

Johnny knew how to entertain a crowd, here he's probably saying 'Can you see me alright?'

Joyce and Johnny.in Acuff's dressing room.

PART 2

KITTY WELLS & JOHNNIE WRIGHT ...

In 1957, Kitty along with Johnnie and Jack, came to Louisville, on a Phillip Morris tour. This was the first time that I met them. Kitty, of course, was and is in my opinion, still the undisputed "Queen" of Country Music! She certainly paved the way for the female artists that have come along since she had her first big hits. Now I know that Patsy Montana had a million-selling recording of a 1935 song titled "I Wanna Be A Cowboy's Sweetheart," but that was a one-time thing and was more Western-flavored, whereas Kitty just kept putting out country hit after hit, along with her duets with Red Foley, Webb Pierce, Roy Drusky, and others, I can't recall at the moment.

By her hanging in there, it had to be the encouragement needed for the other female artists who would come along. As cited earlier, the song that made Kitty a household name was her reply to Hank Thompson's "Wild Side of Life," titled "It Wasn't God Who Made Honky Tonk Angels." It was the first #1 by a country female vocalist.

Johnnie, who has been married to Kitty 72 years, was also the *Johnnie* of the famed RCA country duet, Johnnie & Jack. They put out so many wonderful hits back in the 1950's, some of which are being re-recorded today by new artists, notably "Ashes of Love" and "Stop the World (And Let Me Off)." Another favorite of mine was "Poison Love," Johnnie & Jack's breakthrough hit in 1951.

Sadly, Jack Anglin was killed in a car accident on the way to the prayer service for Patsy Cline on March 7, 1963. Jack was also Johnnie's brother-in-law. In 1962, I met Johnnie and Kitty's daughter Ruby, when they again came to Louisville for the State Fair. I had gone there with Teddy and Doyle Wilburn, as they were on the same show as Johnnie and Kitty. Ruby and her brother Bobby, were singers and were acts in their own right within the family show. Since that time, Ruby and I became good friends and because we were, I got to know Johnnie and Kitty very well.

A good friend of mine at that time, Stu Basore, landed a job with Johnnie and Kitty, as part of their Tennessee Mountain Boys band. Stu later became my brother-in-law and still is. He's married to Marsha. I introduced them when she had come to Nashville on vacation and stayed with me. Stu has worked with many greats in the music industry, including Louie Armstrong.

In 1986, Kitty celebrated 50 years as an entertainer and in October 1987, she and Johnny celebrated 50 years of marriage. Ruby, Bobby, their children, my sisters, Glenda and Marsha and me along with a few others all got together and tossed a big party for them in their home. It was covered by *The Nashville Network* (TNN) and proved to be a great deal of fun. Many from the industry attended the celebration. I made the cake and it even got on national television, but all of us prepared the food. We all had such a good time and what a memory. No one else can say they made a cake for Kitty Wells and Johnnie Wright's 50th Wedding Anniversary!

Marsha always prepares Christmas Eve dinner and you just never know who all is going to show up. One year, she invited Johnnie and Kitty and they came. Ruby always came and before Ruby got ill, she would have the Christmas morning breakfast. It was such a festive time with much sharing and caring going on. We also have had get-togethers at Thanksgiving and the 4th of July. Most of them have been at Glenda's house and again, you never know who would show up. I just came with a dish in hand, *ha!* Charlie Dick is also usually there.

I remember so many times on Christmas night when several of us would go to Kitty and Johnnie's house for refreshments and sometimes even be there for dinner. It was always so much fun. I am so honored to have known and been a friend all these many years with such country legends as you, Kitty and Johnnie, surely are.

When Katherine Sutcliffe, my writer friend, came to town, she along with me and Ruby went to the Country Music Hall of Fame where Kitty is an inductee, then later we went to see Mae Axton and had lunch with her, then on to Kitty's Country Junction Museum. Think about it, here I am in the company of the Queen of Country Music, the "Mama" of Country Music, the daughter of the Queen, and a *New York Times* best-selling novelist. That ain't too bad for a country girl from Pewee Valley, Ky.

In 1991, NARAS presented Kitty with a Grammy, only it wasn't an ordinary Grammy. It was a Grammy Lifetime Achievement Award, the first for a country female. Congratulations Kitty Wells. You are the Queen of Country Music. Thank you, too, for recording your great 1966 album tribute "Songs Made Famous By Jim Reeves."

Joyce (from left), Johnnie Wright, Marsha Basore, Mrs. Wright, and Glenda Stavinoga at Marsha's house, Christmas Eve.

Mae Axton, Kitty, Katherine Sutcliffe, Ruby Taylor and Joyce.

Flanking Kitty are Joyce and Werdna Moss.

Kitty and Mae in Memphis for 'Journey to Graceland' statue unveiling.

At Marsha & Stu Basore's home one Christmas Eve: Johnnie, Kitty and Charlie Dick.

Johnnie & Jack, RCA's 1950s' hitmaking duo.

Joyce was tricked into making her own 50th birthday cake, thinking it was for Kitty's 50th year in music.

RUBY WRIGHT TAYLOR ...

Many of you will remember Ruby as part of the Johnnie & Jack-Kitty Wells' Family Show. Ruby, or course, is Johnnie and Kitty's daughter; however, at one time she was also a solo artist in her own right, as well as part of the RCA group 'Nita, Rita and Ruby. The 'Nita was Anita Carter and Rita was Rita Robbins. All are now deceased.

Ruby and Joyce at Ruby's house.

As stated in the story on Johnnie and Kitty, I first met Ruby in 1962, when she played the Kentucky State Fair with her Mom and Dad. We really didn't get to know each other until Stu Basore, my friend and future brother-in-law, became a member of their band in 1964. We all started visiting when time permitted and a long and wonderful friendship developed.

As I said in my dedication, Ruby was my adopted sister and she has been like one of my sisters all these many years. Not only is she like a sister, but a friend in every sense of the word. She continued to love me and be my friend even with all my shortcomings and believe me, I have many! We have done so much together that it's hard to know what to start with. She and I could have fun doing almost anything, but some of the most fun we had in our earlier years was when we'd get together to have our hair bleached!

Marsha was a hairdresser and we were all blondes (from the bottle) at that time. Marsha would bleach our hair when needed, and we'd make those times into party time! Marsha did hair for many of the artists back then and did the styles for the movie "Second Fiddle To A Steel Guitar." When Marsha and Stu married, Ruby was part of the wedding party, along with myself and two other sisters, Jan and Glenda. Our kids have grown up together and whenever there are family gatherings, she was always a part of them. We always did fun things like Charades, Win, Lose or Draw, Trivial Pursuit or just sitting around having coffee and talking.

Ruby and I always loved historical romance novels and many of these were set in New Orleans. Ruby wanted me and her to go there, and on Thanksgiving Day 1989, after we had eaten our dinner, we went. This was the Thanksgiving after my mom had passed away in June. We had a marvelous time. It was so much fun seeing and being at the places that I had only read about. You could feel the history emanating all around you, especially in Jackson Square. If you enjoy reading the way we do, seeing a place that you've read about makes it more realistic. We had both been to England, though not together, and many of the books we read have had England as a setting. We never lacked for conversation when we were together, as we had so much in common.

Joyce and Ruby laugh it up during a 'bleach' job.

Over the years we exchanged books that we liked to read. It was a thing of ours to give each other whatever book we were looking for, and not buy it for ourselves, but allow it to be a gift from each other. It was just our thing.

On my birthday in 1990, none of our favorite authors had books out, but knowing the kind of books that we enjoyed reading, Ruby read on the back cover of this particular book that she was thinking about buying for me, and it looked like one that we would enjoy, so she bought it and gave it to me rather reluctantly. I read it and thoroughly enjoyed it. In fact, I enjoyed it so much that I decided that I would write a letter to the author, letting her know that I had enjoyed her book, and that I was an avid reader of her particular style of writing - and after reading this book, I classified her among the others that had become our favorites.

I didn't want her to think me a complete nut, so I gave her a little history of myself. She answered my letter and to make a long story short, we all became extremely good friends, and all because of the book that Ruby reluctantly gave me. The book, by the way, was titled "A Fire In the Heart" by Katherine Sutcliffe.

Ruby and I always enjoyed going to the movies together and when we'd find one we really liked, we might see it three or four times. I know that's how it was with "Dances With Wolves." Wow! We loved that movie. I think we saw it about three times at the theater, and then she later bought the movie and we watched it again at home. I also have the VHS of it now, and still watch it from time to time.

When my Mom got sick and passed on, Ruby was right there for all of us to lean on. She and her daughter Corrie sang at Mom's funeral. In fact, I know that I am the most blessed person in all the world when it comes to having friends. They each helped me through the most traumatic times of my life in their own individual way, and when

Ruby and Joyce enjoy their get-away in New Orleans.

Ruby, author Katherine Sutcliffe and Joyce at the Broadway Dinner Train in Nashville.

you have friends like that sometimes you forget to say *thank you* and let them know how much they are appreciated, so thank you to each of you - you know who you are.

Like I said, Ruby was always there. You could count on her through the sad times, the bad times, the good times and just any ole time! Ruby, if I didn't say it enough how much I appreciate you, I am doing so now. I loved you like a sister and I loved you as my friend. You have always believed in me and have freely given your encouragement to me during the writing of this book. I will miss you so much. (Ruby died on Sept. 27, 2009, from a heart attack. It was exactly one month prior to her 70th birthday.) I love you, my friend.

TEDDY · DECCA RECORDS · DOYLE

THE WILBURN BROTHERS ...

I have to go all the way back to 1954, the year I first met Teddy and Doyle Wilburn, and that really taxes my memory, but I will try.

They were playing the Armory in Louisville, and being the fan that I was, I just had to go see them. My sister Glenda and a good friend, Maggie Ott Koontz, went with me. Now I don't know how I managed to get backstage, but somehow I talked my way back there. I think I fell in love with both of them the moment we finally met.

Mainly because they were filled with charm and a little B.S. I guess, but I bought whatever they told me. Notably how much they appreciated my coming to the show and all the same things they tell everyone, but that night as far as I was concerned, they spoke to me alone! From that night on, I went to every concert they were a part of in the Louisville area, and there were several. The more they saw me, the friendlier they became and, of course, this didn't hurt my feelings any! I liked the idea that they would say hello to me from the stage or say it was OK for the security guards to let me backstage.

So the friendship began and when I moved to Nashville (Doyle tried to talk me out of moving, as he was afraid I'd get mixed up with, as he put it, some of the wrong *hillbillies*), Teddy and Doyle were really the only people I knew in town - and I didn't know them very well. We did have some mutual friends, who had lived in Nashville, but they moved away in November before I moved there in January. One mutual friend was Shirley Valliere Johnson, who was secretary to Faron Young, and his manager-booking agent Hubert Long. Hubert died Sept. 7, 1972, but he contributed so very much to the music industry, and it was an honor knowing him.

Shirley and her roommates, Coleen Johnson Ruperto and Joyce Swanson, had invited me to come to the DJ Convention in November 1957. I had met them on three different occasions during that year on my Nashville visits. I knew when I arrived for the convention that they were planning to move at the end of that month.

It wasn't long after I moved that I met "Mom" and "Pop" Wilburn, and we became pretty good friends. I was also getting to know Ted and Doyle much better. I remember going over to The Wilburns on weekends and Mom would make breakfast. She would and did cook for about everyone at one time or another. I would venture to say that she cooked for all the music people of that time period. She was a sweet, loving lady. Both she and Pop are gone now.

Teddy, Lester and Leslie (Lester and Leslie were the older brothers) all enjoyed bowling. Lester died in 1990 from a heart attack. It wasn't long until bowling also became one of my favorite sports, too! What better way to be around and get to know some of your favorite people a little more? Besides being a lot of fun, it brought us a lot closer as friends and we spent a great deal of spare time in various bowling alleys. The closer we became as friends, the less I thought of them as anything other than that, except I had a tremendous crush on Doyle that started when we first met.

Doyle very seldom joined in with us on our nights at the bowling alley or on the Sundays when we would gather at Edwin Warner Park to play softball. He missed out on some really good times, but there were also some special times for me where Doyle was concerned. One of those times was when a group of artists such as Doyle, Porter Wagoner, Don Gibson and others would rent a hotel or motel room where they could play poker all night. I was fortunate enough to be invited to some of these by Doyle. I think he asked me so I could mix them drinks and make sandwiches. I didn't care because I was with him. Once the playing began, they would not leave the table except for an occasional trip to the bathroom. Other girls were along, but you know I never saw any *hanky panky* going on between anyone. I've wondered about that as I have grown older. Like I said, I was invited by Doyle and he thought of me and treated me like a big brother, but I'm sure the others did not have this same kind of relationship with who invited them.

Back in 1959, Ted and Doyle asked my friend Joyce Caperton Chinique and I to go with them to Meridian, Miss., to attend the Jimmie Rodgers Memorial Day Celebration. Wow! Were we ever thrilled. I still had my big crush on Doyle and Joyce had one on Teddy, and this was just too good to be true! If my memory serves me correctly, they sat in the front seat and we sat in the back the entire trip. I know we were extremely disappointed, but were too naïve to suggest a change in the seating arrangement. Actually, we were just happy to be that close to them for such a long time. We had a lot of fun and met a lot of people in the industry.

This was where I first met Ferlin Husky, whose hits included "Wings Of a Dove."

I was very fortunate to be invited to go on several trips with many of the artists that I had become friends with.

A trip with Teddy and Doyle that stands out in my mind was in 1962. It was to Louisville's Freedom Hall during the Kentucky State Fair. They though it would be a good time for me to see my Mom since she lived nearby. My Mom and sister Marsha (she hadn't yet moved to Nashville) came out to see the show and, of course, to see me. We had some time to kill before the show began and Ted asked if Marsha and I would like to go out on the Midway. Mom and Doyle were in deep conversation (she loved Doyle and he loved her, too) at any rate, so we told Ted that we'd like to go with him. George Jones was within hearing distance and I might add, feeling no pain. He asked if he could go with us. It didn't matter to us, so the four of us headed out on the Midway. We got to a ride called "The Wild Mouse" and thought it would be fun to ride. What we didn't know was that George was deathly afraid to ride any kind of ride, but being somewhat inebriated, he braved it and got on with Marsha. Now it isn't hard to figure out who I rode with, is it? If you have never ridden a "Wild Mouse," you should! It jerks you around a great deal and even though they are a bit scary, they are a lot of fun. When it stopped, George was as white as a ghost! He got down and kissed the ground and said, "Never again will I ever get on anything like that. I thought it was all over and that I would never get back to Nashville to make another record."

One of the most memorable evenings that I have ever had was spent with Doyle. It was after the *Friday Night Frolics.* Doyle asked me to go to his office, which was only a couple of doors down from the *Frolics.* His office was in the old Masonic Lodge Building, and he had some songs he wanted me to hear, and after we had listened for quite some time, he asked if I would like to go out and do the town. Well, he might have treated me like a big brother, but I still had my crush on him, so naturally, I jumped at the chance to go anywhere with him. We went everywhere. He took me to the Rainbow Room, a strip joint and we sat right up front. I think Doyle knew the stripper!

It was the first time that I had ever been in a place like that and come to think of it, I don't think I have been in one since. I didn't care because I was with Doyle and it didn't matter where we were. I was safe with him and I knew it. We went to some places where they rolled dice or shot craps or whatever it's called. I don't remember where it was, but it was in an upstairs room and they knew Doyle, so it was OK. Gambling was illegal then, as it is now in Tennessee. We left there and went to a place called The Uptown Club. They knew him there also, so we had no trouble. I got the impression that they were careful who they let into those places. It was very late when we got home, but I finally got my night out with Doyle, and it was one that I will never forget, because not only was I with him which was so special, but I was introduced to a Nashville I was unfamiliar with. Those places don't exist any longer.

When Doyle took me home, he said, "Now you've been all over town and I hope I never catch you anywhere near those places again." He never did, because I never went! Teddy had all the girls crazy about him, but he didn't really date any of them, which is why they were all after him I suppose. I loved him, but only as a friend. He was so evasive. No one knew what he did or where he went. I know there were many times when us girls would try to find out where he was going, after he would leave wherever we all had been. We even went as far as trying to follow him. He always lost us! I sure had some fun times with him at the bowling alleys. There was, and I think still is, a place called Strike and Spare, where we would go and bowl all night. They called it Midnight Bowl.

My Mom and Dad always thought the world of all the Wilburns and when they would come to Nashville for a visit, they would go out to the park with us for those wonderful softball games mentioned earlier. We never knew just who would be at the park to participate. There would be people like Justin Tubb (who actually started us going), Lester and Leslie, Mel Tillis, Wayne Walker and Elaine (Elaine is Justin's sister and they're children of Ernest Tubb. Elaine was then married to Wayne), Dottie West and her family, John Denny and anyone else who wanted to be part of a good time.

We pooled our money for whatever we wanted to eat. I know one time that really stands out to me was when Hank Locklin was in town for the Opry, and he stayed over and joined us on Sunday at the park. The park opened at 9 a.m. and closed around 11 p.m. We'd play softball and cook out during the day, and off-and-on during the day we'd gather wood for a big bonfire for that night. On the night Hank had joined us, we had our fire going and had finished our hamburgers and hot dogs and were roasting marshmallows when someone got out their guitar (there was always someone with a guitar) and began singing. This wasn't unusual, but it was a beautiful warm night, clear and the moon was just coming up over the trees that surrounded us and Hank took the guitar and sang "Send Me the Pillow You Dream On." I tell you that song has never been sung by anyone as well as it was that night! It was something that is just unforgettable! Today when I see the moon coming up over the trees, I recall that special night and Hank. It's just one of those things that you plant somewhere in your memory that surfaces from time-to-time. I thank God for this special memory and for knowing Hank Locklin.

Time passed and Doyle married Margie Bowes, and Lester married Linda Todd and Justin was already married and little by little things changed. People's lives change and our little group sorta split up. It was no one's fault, just change, that's all - and for some reason you can never go back and recapture what once was. We talked about going back to the park many times, but no one took the time to organize it and probably everyone would have found an excuse not to go, even if they were contacted, That's life.

Doyle and Margie had one daughter, Sharon. My sister Glenda kept her from the time she was born and for several years after that. Margie was recording and had some pretty big records (one being "Poor Old Heartsick Me"), so she was busy working the road, doing concerts; and, of course, Teddy and Doyle were very busy at that time. (Margie had won the Pet Milk Talent Contest and received a recording contract.)

We all fell in love with "Baby Sharon" who is now all grown up with a daughter named Katie after "Mom" Wilburn, and recently became a grandmother herself. She never got into the music business, but she should have, as she sings beautifully. When Glenda's daughter Robin got married they asked Sharon to sing at their wedding. She sang a duet with a friend of hers from church, titled "Just You and I," and you could have heard a pin drop. It was just beautiful!

Margie is no longer in the business. Doyle had to be hospitalized in 1982. He had the dreaded cancer and on Oct. 16, 1982, died. I feel that Doyle really made a difference during his lifetime in the industry and otherwise. He and Teddy were among the first to have heir own TV show, which, of course, had guest artists on each week. These artists got exposure and coverage from that show they normally would not have gotten. They not only helped the new artist, but let the world share the big name artists, as well.

Doyle was the first in Nashville to recognize the talent of Loretta Lynn and anyone who goes back that far cannot dispute this fact. I remember meeting Loretta, either the first or second night she was in town. It was on a Saturday night and Teddy and Doyle brought her to Ernest Tubb's *Midnight Jamboree,* held at Ernest Tubb's Record Shop downtown. That's where it all started for Loretta. Doyle and Teddy took her under their wing and helped to develop the Loretta that we all know and love today.

When Doyle got so sick that he had to have someone with him most of the time while even in the hospital, it was a time when I felt so helpless. I called Linda (Lester's wife) and asked her if there was anything at all that I could do for them. I knew I really couldn't do anything for Doyle and that was frustrating within itself. She told me that I could give them a break by coming to the hospital and staying with Doyle.

Thank God I did that! I remember him telling me that he was going to beat it and that he had made his peace with God. I choose to think that is what he meant by saying that he was going to beat it! I loved you Doyle and there are times now when we talk about you, that our loss is just as painful as it was then. I think that one of the things that endeared you to me was the fact that you loved my sweet little Mom, and boy, did she ever love you two guys. This is hard for me to write, Doyle, but I hope you and Mom are having some of those wonderful conversations now.

Doyle, you'd be pleased to know that your friends loved you. What a crowd there was at your funeral. In fact, of all the different ones that I have attended, I would say that you had the longest funeral procession of them all. Doyle is buried at the National Cemetery on Gallatin Road in Madison. My sister Glenda's husband Bob was one of the pallbearers.

Joyce, Teddy and Joyce Caperton Chinique.

One of the last get-togethers between my family and the Wilburns was at Glenda's house. Doyle said he'd come if someone would fix pinto beans and cornbread. We were all going to bring a dish so no one person would have to do all the cooking. I brought the pinto beans and cornbread! We all had such a good time looking at pictures and reminiscing about all the fun times together.

Ted made many appearances as a solo act both on the road and on the Opry, but was just never the same after Doyle died. Ted pretty much became a recluse, but when Jeanie and Frank Oakley were setting up The Willie Nelson Museum, I called Ted and asked him for something of his and Doyle's to go into the museum. Ted told us to come over to his house and Frank and I did, and he gave us one of their beautiful Nudie suits for the museum. They're still in the museum today.

Ted joined Doyle, Nov. 24, 2003. When I think back to one of the most fun times that I ever shared with Ted (other than our Sundays at the park), what comes to mind is when we took Patsy Cline, Charlie Dick and Betty Jacobs (B.Z.) to Melrose Bowling Lanes one night when they had come to Nashville. We bowled all night long. It wasn't the first time that I met Patsy, but it was when I felt that I first got to know her.

Doyle, Joyce and Teddy in 1954.

Joyce and Doyle.

Maggie Ott Koontz, the Wilburns and Glenda, Joyce's sister.

Doyle, Joyce and Teddy.

Doyle and Teddy.

Doyle and Joyce.

Doyle and Teddy with Shirley Valliere Johnson.

Teddy and Doyle with Joyce.

Wilburn brothers: Lester, Doyle, Teddy and Leslie.

Teddy with Joyce Caperton Chinique and Joyce.

Doyle, Jerry Reed and Teddy Wilburn.

Doyle and Joyce.

Leslie Wilburn, Sharon Begin Lange and Joyce.

Doyle and Joyce.

Leslie died in January 2005. The only one left of the original Wilburn family is Geraldine, their only sister, who lives in Arkansas where they were originally from. Thanks for the good times Ted, Doyle, Lester and Leslie . . .We sure had a lot of 'em! You both should be in the Country Music Hall of Fame, as you've helped the industry so much.

Joyce and Doyle.

EDDY ARNOLD ...

I was a fan of Eddy Arnold for many years before we finally met. I remember being mad when Eddie Fisher came out covering Eddy's 1948 hit "Anytime." Eddy Arnold had it out first, so back then I thought the song belonged to him exclusively. It was a hit for Fisher also in the pop chart, and while the kids in my school were raving about his version, I was singing Eddy Arnold's praises, as I felt he had the best recording of that song, and still do!

Eddy attended the DJ Convention of 1958, in the Andrew Jackson Hotel, and we met in the RCA suite. Back in the late 1950's and early 1960's, Nashville had a minor league baseball team,The Nashville Vols, and the games were played at the Sulphur Dell Stadium (no longer there). Jim Reeves had box seats, but when he was out of town, I took advantage of his box seats and went to as many home games as I possibly could. That's when I really got to know Eddy. He had box seats also and I would see him at the games and we'd always have some great conversations. He found out that I was from a little place near Louisville called Pewee Valley and that I knew where LaGrange, Ky., was. His wife Sally was from LaGrange. I went to school with her brother. We weren't in the same class, just the same school and, of course, being a fan of country music, I knew who he was. All of us did. Because of that fact, Eddy and I had something in common to talk about and later when I met Sally, it was a good topic of conversation for us.

Eddy and Jim's voices have often been compared, but frankly, I could never hear the comparison, except that they both sang slow ballads, but in my opinion they each had their own style of delivering a song - and both did it well.

When Jim got killed and search parties were looking for his and Dean's bodies, Eddy reportedly was in the party that found him and made an on-the-scene identification, and as I have stated earlier in this book, I don't see how that could have been, as I made the official identification and I know what I had to go on, and don't see how Eddy could have done it, but that's what the papers said.

Jim and Eddy were both on RCA, so naturally they attended many of the same RCA-hosted receptions. I was fortunate enough to be able to attend some of these as well, and feel that I got to know both the artist and the person of Eddy Arnold by being around him at the ballgames and these label functions.

I also saw a great deal of Eddy in the RCA Building during the early 1970's. It was during this time that his son had a head-on car wreck that nearly killed him. His recovery was a lengthy one. That is when I knew of the strong faith and deep courage that Eddy has within.

I called on Eddy when I was collecting personal items for the Hands Across The Table celebrity auction, which was held in Billings. Like so many others, he gave freely for this cause.

Eddy was elected to the Country Music Hall of Fame in 1966, and rightly so! He is another legend that I can call friend, and I'm honored to be able to do so. Eddy always treated me the same whether it was at a Sulphur Dell ballgame, at an RCA event or a mutual friend's house (Charlie Moseley's) for a party. I thank both him and Sally for always making me feel a little special.

Thinking of Sally makes me recall the opening of The Jim Reeves Museum. We were having a private opening for people in the music business, plus tourist-related businesses. I was helping direct people to the front of the museum and putting name tags on them. I looked up and here comes Sally and Eddy. When Sally got to where I was, she said, "I was sweeping off my back porch the other day and I got to thinking about you and wondered where you were now." I have never been able to figure out how her sweeping off her back porch brought me to her mind!

When Katherine Sutcliffe came to Nashville, I had the pleasure of introducing her to Eddy Arnold at the airport, when she was on her way back home. She and Eddy were booked on the same flight that was heading for Dallas. As fate would have it, Eddy and Sally died within weeks of each other in 2008.

MARTY ROBBINS ...

It was somewhere around 1957, as Marty came to Louisville to either the Armory or to Freedom Hall at the fairgrounds when we met. After moving to Nashville, I got to know him a little better, but not as well as I did so many of the other entertainers. Marty was one of my favorite singers and Jim Reeves always listed Marty as his favorite country singer. I even have a few of his earlier recordings on the old 78rpm speed that I treasure!

Throughout this book, I have mentioned Linebaugh's Restaurant. Once the Opry moved from the Ryman out to the Opry House, Linebaugh's became a thing of the past, and they've even torn it down. I know there are some of you that share with me some of the wonderful memories and friendships established there.

Marty is such a vital part of this memorable past, when I recall the time spent in this gathering place! There was a jukebox right in the center of the restaurant and I can't tell you the times that Marty would come in say hello to everyone, walk over to that jukebox and play every record that they had on it by him, and then just walk out the door. We had no choice but to listen to at least six of his recordings. Sometimes he would join us for a Coke or coffee, or whatever he was drinking, but he never stayed any length of time like the rest of us did. He'd play the pinball machine at times, but he always seemed to be in a hurry to get somewhere else.

One night Bud Wingard (a writer of the *Hee Haw* TV show) invited a group of entertainers and others in the music business to his house for Mexican food. I was happily included on his guest list. What I didn't know at the time was that Marty was the one cooking the Mexican food. It was wonderful! He was a terrific cook! I accused him of having his wife Marizona cook it to bring it over to Charlie's. She probably did help. There was a great deal of taco meat left over after everyone was through with the meal and Marty asked if I would like to have the leftover meat. Since Marty was offering, I said yes and he gave it to me in a Tupperware container. I'm sure it was one of Marizona's. I still have that piece of Tupperware! I know I should have given it back, but I just never did, and I keep my cornmeal in it to this day. If Marizona wanted it back, I would have returned it, but my meal would never have been the same.

Another fond memory that I have of Marty is one day I ran into him on the street and we stood for the longest time and talked and talked. We talked about Jim and he told me how he had admired Jim's talent. He even said that Jim was his favorite male country singer. I know there was a professional rivalry between these two greats, but I feel they really did respect each other as entertainers.

Ralph Emery mentioned to me when he was writing his book, whether I felt if they liked each other or not, and I related to him what I knew of Jim's admiration for Marty. He made that notation in his book and I'm glad that he did, as I would not want the public to think that healthy competition between such talented artists would be mistaken for dislike.

Marty was fortunate enough to be elected to the Country Music Hall of Fame (Oct. 18, 1982), just before his death, Dec. 8, 1982. He deserved to be a Hall of Fame member, because Marty, you were more than a singer, you were an entertainer in every sense of the word. You are missed not only because of your ability to sing, but because you were always fun to be around. I didn't know you very well, but I treasure what little I did know you, and I thank you and Marizona for the Tupperware!

Marty and Joyce.

Marty performs with his band in 1957.

JEAN SHEPARD ...

Jean Shepard and I became friends almost immediately. Her sister, Frances, was living with her at the time we met shortly after I came down from Louisville. She was living in East Nashville and my sister Glenda and I helped her move to the home she bought on Bell Grimes Lane.

That is where she was living when Hawkshaw was killed. Even before that, I went on several trips with Jean. One that I remember in particular was to East Point, Ga., near Atlanta. I believe the theater had been an old school converted into a theater and many of the country artists played there. I know that Leo Jackson came to the show to see Jean. He was still in the Army and was at Ft. McPherson near East Point. I don't know how Leo got to the show, but Jean let me take her car and drive him back to the base, and that is where I got my first kiss from him!

Another time that Jean let me use her car was after Glenda moved to Nashville and we wanted to go home and see Mom and Dad one weekend, but didn't have a way. On the first Thanksgiving after I moved to Nashville, Jean went home with us and had Thanksgiving with my entire family. We had such a good time and they loved her. She loved them, too, and as long as Mom was alive, I don't think I ever saw Jean that she failed to ask how Mom was.

It was about this same Thanksgiving time that she and her steady Hawkshaw were having problems, and Jody McCrea was in town. He really liked Jean and they saw a great deal of each other for a short period of time. She also renewed her relationship with Doyle Wilburn briefly. I know Doyle loved Jean, as he told me so himself. He proved how much he cared when Jean got very ill, and we had to call an ambulance and rush her to the hospital.

Hawkshaw didn't like it at all that Doyle was at the hospital and called me on the phone at work and got on my case really bad about it. I remember telling him that I had no say in who Jean had as friends, and he told me that if I was really her friend, I would not let her associate with Doyle or anyone else, because he was the only one who really loved her, and that they would be back together. He was right about that. It wasn't long after her hospital stay that they were married. They had two little boys together: Don and Harold. Harold Franklin II was born a month after Hawkshaw was killed (Harold was really Hawk's given name.)

Another trip that I went on with Jean was to Charlotte, N.C. Guitarist Pete Wade was with us. It was a fun trip, as were all the trips with Jean.

Jean is now married to Benny Birchfield and has been for many years. She still works the *Grand Ole Opry* and also works numerous road dates. Whenever I've called on her for one thing or another, she has always come through for me. Jean was among the many stars who donated an article of clothing for the celebrity auction Hands Across The Table.

When I think of Jean and the Opry, I always remember one night that I had gone with her when it was still at the Ryman Auditorium. Jean got someone's raincoat and an old hat and walked out on stage during Teddy and Doyle's performance. It broke everyone up, including the brothers. You just never knew what she'd pull.

Jean was one of many who visited me in the hospital when Joy was born, and brought me a fruit basket in the shape of a bassinet. We used that little basket for a number of years to give showers for expectant moms. Glenda added lace all around it and we used it for favors. When I moved to Colorado, I had to get rid of many things and that basket was one of them.

Jean, I thank you for the way you always treated my Mom and Dad. They always felt you were special and you were, and still are to me. I value our friendship, all the fun trips and all the wonderful memories we have shared.

Glenda said she ran into you recently and the first thing you did was ask about me. Do you even know how precious that is to me? It is, and so are you. I love you, Jean.

Jean with sons Harold II and Don.

Jean enjoys a turkey leg at the Grays' house.

Jean and Hank Snow with Joyce.

Holiday dinner at the Gray house in Kentucky, (from left) Jean, Joyce, mother Sue, nephew Terry Gray, dad Wiley Gray; (standing) sisters Marsha, Janet, and Jean's sister Frances Shepard.

Jean with The Jordanaires: Gordon Stoker, Hoyt Hawkins, Ray Walker and Neal Matthews.

Jean and Joyce with Ray Price.

Jean, pianist Del Wood and Joyce.

Jean cracked up Doyle and Teddy Wilburn, coming on stage in a raincoat and old hat during their set.

Joyce and Jean by the Opry mail-slots.

Jean and Joyce with Cowboy Copas.

GRANT TURNER ...

The voice of the *Grand Ole Opry,* and what a voice it was. Everyone knew who Grant Turner was, as he did the announcing for the various commercials and when he would bring on a performer.

Many times throughout this book, I've used the word *legend* when describing a person, but it's not a word that I've over-used, because so many of my friends have been and still are legends. Mr. Grant certainly deserves to be in that category. I can't stress enough how fortunate and how honored I am to have been associated with and yes, even been good friends with many of the legends.

Grant Turner was always very cooperative whether it be my arranging to have him in one of Jim's fan club journals or if asked for a charitable item or donation. He was always ready to help in whatever you might want him to do. No matter where or when you saw Mr. Grant, he was always the same. If he was having a bad day, he never showed it, at least I never saw it and I was around him quite a bit, especially during my earlier years with him.

I think one of the things that impressed me the most about him was his incredible memory. He always remembered your name and always made you feel genuinely welcome whether it be at the *Grand Ole Opry* or another function that he was attending. In 1989, Mr. Grant was given the Ernest Tubb Humanitarian Award during the R.O.P.E. (Reunion of Professional Entertainers) Banquet, given to a person for outstanding contributions to the betterment of the music industry and in their helpfulness to individuals in this industry.

Mr. Grant was fortunate enough to be able to celebrate over 50 years in an industry that he loved so much and I believe that it was in 1944, when he came to Nashville and became a part of WSM radio and the Opry as their announcer. I feel that when we lost him in the fall of 1991, we lost the voice of WSM, one in my opinion that can never be replaced and he is truly missed by not only his peers, but his listeners as well. Mr. Grant was inducted into the Country Music Hall of Fame, Oct. 12, 1981, and I'm so glad that he was able to enjoy this honor that was bestowed upon him.

My life in Nashville was made richer with my having known Grant Turner. God surely blessed me when he allowed our paths to cross and I still miss him. (Grant Turner died Oct. 19,1991.)

WSM's Grant Turner, a member of the DJ Hall of Fame, visits with good friend Joyce Jackson backstage at the Opry.

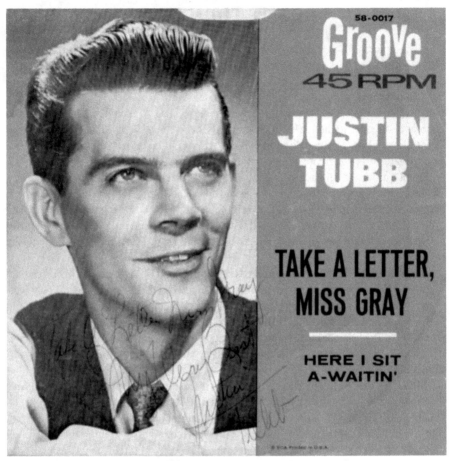

JUSTIN TUBB ...

I'd known Justin for so long that it seemed like I knew him all my life. I have known him for more years than I haven't!

I can remember listening to the *Midnight Jamboree* for many years before I finally moved to Nashville, and Ernest would have him on as his guest at times. I really met him in March 1957, when I first visited Nashville. Shirley, Faron Young's secretary, introduced me to him down at the Ernest Tubb Record Shop during the *Midnight Jamboree*. (Later, of course, Justin became the regular host of the *Midnight Jamboree*.)

As I said, I went to Linebaugh's a great deal because there was never a time back then that you couldn't run into someone you knew. Most of the time you'd find Justin, the Wilburn brothers (all of them), Floyd Cramer and about any member of the Opry, along with some of us that were just friends.

It was there where Justin organized the Sundays out at Edwin Warner Park for softball and a day of fun and fellowship. It was at Linebaugh's that we all decided that we should begin bowling. We bowled in leagues at Melrose, Strike and Spare and at Donelson Bowling Lane. Justin was an extremely good bowler. Seems we were always having fun doing something or the other in those days.

Justin was then married to Bea Swift and they had a daughter, Leah Lisa (Leah passed away in 2008). They divorced in 1962. He had two sons by Carolyn, his second wife: Gary Justin and Zachary.

Just about the time that he and Bea divorced, Justin really began taking his songwriting more seriously. It was during the 1962 DJ Convention that Justin wrote a song that earned him his very first songwriting award. It was called "Take A Letter, Miss Gray." He had been trying to write it as "Take a Letter, Miss Smith" when Joe Allison suggested that Justin use my last name, Gray. This was my maiden name. So Justin substituted Miss Gray for Miss Smith and came up with the song that won him his award. Justin had been saying many things that would either be good song titles or good lines to put in a song during this convention, and I began writing them down for him, so he might use them after it was over, which gave Joe the idea for him to use *Miss Gray.*

Justin recorded it himself and it was released on RCA's subsidiary label, Groove Records. When released, the label had put a sheet of shorthand steno pad paper in it with all the information about the record in shorthand. Justin asked me if I would go with him to the Ralph Emery all-night radio show to get his record reviewed, since my name was involved. I did go with Justin and Ralph had me read all about the record from the sheet of shorthand paper over the air. I believe that Justin and I established our real friendship during that 1962 Convention.

Justin was very despondent because of his divorce and was drinking a great deal and popping uppers. He and I spent a lot of time in the Liberty Records Hospitality Suite. I was more or less just watching after him, as I felt he needed someone around that cared about him. He knew he wasn't sober enough to really know what he was doing, so he gave me his car keys and asked me to keep them for him. He said if he had them, he'd let someone have his car and it would be no telling when he'd get it back or in what condition.

Many different artists came by the suite to visit with Joe, who was A&R director for Liberty Records at that time, and with all of us who were there. I don't remember who all came by, but I remember that Bobby Bare stopped by and Warren Smith. I also remember that Warren was upset because he had played some date and evidently was supposed to be the star that closed the show, but the promoters or buyers of the show let someone else close instead. I suppose his ego was bruised a bit, because he was complaining a great deal and I think Justin got tired of hearing it and made a statement that I've always thought as just plain classic.

"Warren, I've always thought it wasn't how you went on, but how you come off that counts." I loved it then and I still do today, as I feel it's a very true statement, no matter who you are or what you might be doing. It's how you do it that counts."

Justin must have stayed in that suite for at least two days and nights. I'd go home long enough to shower, change clothes and come back, as I was afraid to leave him for long. He finally said he had to go somewhere, but that he didn't want to go home, so I told him he could come home with me and I would make him some breakfast and he could at least shower and get cleaned up. He agreed finally to come home with me. I told him to lie on the couch while I made breakfast. He fell asleep and since he needed it so badly, I just let him sleep. When he did wake up, he was feeling terrible. He was hung over, had a headache and was just miserable. The sun was shining through the front door and that gave him an idea for another song, which he wrote right then called

"Sorry 'Bout That World Out There." I don't know if it has ever been recorded or not, but I sure do like that song.

After he ate a little breakfast and had some coffee, he began to feel human again, but still didn't want to go to his house, so he asked me if I would drive him to a few different places and get him some new clothes to put on. Of course, I said I would. He gave me his wallet and told me the places he wanted me to go and I outfitted him from his socks to his shirt. He was very trusting, as he had quite a bit of money in that wallet and he just handed it over to me, so I could pay for all the items he wanted. He would stay in the car and I'd go into the various stores and purchase what he wanted. It's hard to believe that all took place over 40 years ago.

It was also about this time that Justin wrote "Love Is No Excuse." Some friends had gathered at Dottie and Bill West's house. We did that a lot back then. I remember Justin lying in the middle of Dottie's living room floor writing that particular song. Dottie recorded it as a duet with Jim Reeves and it became a big hit record.

Justin, like most of us, has had both highs and lows in his life, but I know that one of his highs had to be when the group Highway 101 released one of Justin's songs titled "Walkin', Talkin', Cryin', Barely Beatin' Broken Heart." Credits show Roger Miller as co-writer of this song, but I happen to know that Justin wrote all of it and put Roger's name on it. If I'm not mistaken, Roger did the same thing for Justin on one of his songs. (Incidentally, newly solo and newly named - Johnny - Wright was the first to record that song, a Top 20 for Decca in 1964.)

I was invited and went to Justin's 50th birthday party that David McCormick gave for him, and I was so glad to see that Justin was happy and things seemed to be going well in his life again. He's been mentioned several times throughout this book and rightly so, as we all did so much together during those early years, softball, bowling, and our get-togethers from time to time, all of which Justin organized. Justin started giving us all the nicknames, which I've included in this book.

Looking back, I feel we just took all that Justin did for granted when really they made for many wonderful and beautiful memories. God, how I wish I'd kept a diary. Justin, your friendship has been such a wonderful part of my Nashville years and up until the time that you went home to be with the Lord, not one of those years was spent without you being involved in some way. I know I never did let you know just how important you were to me, but I'm now letting everyone else know that you were so very special to me.

Justin sent both Christmas and birthday cards to me and missed very few of either of them. I have most of them today. When Justin passed away, I was at the funeral home for visitation and the directors just didn't have his hair right or his glasses on right and as Carolyn and I were viewing him, I made that comment and she agreed and took out her comb and asked me to fix his hair and straighten his glasses. I was happy to do that and he looked more like himself after I finished.

Justin, I miss the Christmas cards, the birthday cards, the softball games, the bowling, the get-togethers, the years of friendship and Justin, I'll "Take A Letter . . . " from you any day! (Justin died Jan. 24, 1998.)

This is a copy of a *thank you* note that Justin wrote to me after we had attended a surprise 50th birthday party for him, hosted by David McCormick. The reason he signed it "Simply John" was because that is how the song "Take A Letter, Miss Gray" ended.

DEAR Joyce -
    THANKS A MILLION TO you & Joy
FOR COMING TO my PARTY. I'VE
NEVER BEEN AS SURPRISED IN my LIFE.
IT'S A NIGHT I'll LONG REMEMBER.
    AND THE BEAUTIFUL SILVER GUITAR
WAS SO THOUGHTFUL. I will
TREASURE IT ALWAYS!
    AND, OH YES,
    P.S.
THANKS FOR BEING my FRIEND!
        Justin
        (SIMPLY, JOHN)

Justin and Joyce, the 'Miss Gray' in his hit song.

NICKNAMES OF THE 1960's

These are the names that Justin gave to various people on the music scene. If you didn't like the name, then that's who you became:

Ralph Emery - Mumcrief
Skeeter Davis - Justerini (Deceased)
Marvis Thompson - Prudence
Terry Bethel - Flea
Red Lane - Schmedley
Glen Campbell - Humbolt
Lee Hazlewood - Chitwood (Deceased)
Happy Wilson - Dunlap (Deceased)
Steve Sholes - Faircloth (Deceased)
Joyce Gray Jackson - Gladys
Cousin Jody - Cromwell (Deceased)
Cal Everhart - Bascomb
Hank Cochran - Goodacre
Dottie West - Beulah (Deceased)
Bill West - Orville
Charlie Dick - Spaulding/Moby
Bob Holt - Julius
Dottie Holt - Agnes
Carl Perkins - Coleridge (Deceased)
Justin Tubb - Proctor (Deceased)
Billy Graves - Orson
Rusty Kershaw - Wharton
Doug Kershaw - Lovelace
Ben Dorsey - Poot
Tommy Hill - Arbuckle (Deceased)
Carolyn Endiman (Sells) - Opal
Chet Atkins - Prentiss (Deceased)
Robert Riley - Armstrong (Deceased)
Billy Grammer - Cameron
Larry Lee - Murphy
Ray Price - Guthrie
Willie Nelson - Osgood
Shirley Nelson - Edna
Billy Tubb - Rhinehart
Butch Tubb - Sapphire
Joe Allison - Ballard (Deceased)
Tommy Allsup - Nesbett
Roger Miller - Sweeney (Deceased)
Wayne Walker - Whitney (Deceased)
Elaine Walker - Chloe
Gene King -Schwartz
Mel Tillis - Doolittle
Billy Walker - Tugwell (Deceased)

Buddy Killen- Childress (Deceased)
Bobby Sykes - Rutledge (Deceased)
Bob Olsen - Hornsby
Bobby Bare - Andwrite
Bobby Lord - Rigsby (Deceased)
Jeannie Seely - Dabney
Jerry Shook - Wooten
Pete Drake - Rose (Deceased)
Kelso Hurston - Sport
June Vaupel Glaser - Grisselda

LARRY GATLIN ...

There isn't a great deal for me to write about where Larry Gatlin is concerned, but I remember him best from his early years in Nashville. Dottie West had just recently brought Larry to town, and I happened to be at her house one night when Larry was there. Dottie introduced us. (He had been a member of The Imperials vocal group that often backed Elvis Presley.)

Dottie thought Larry was one of the finest writers that she had ever met. I remember she was very high on him and his talent (he is a great writer and one of my favorites is "Leave The Leaving to Someone Else.").

I saw him a few weeks after that night at Dottie's, in the back parking lot of the RCA Building. I had left my office on the way to lunch when I heard someone yelling at me. It was Larry. He had remembered meeting me at Dottie's. He re-introduced himself to me, but I told him that I remembered meeting him. We chatted for a moment and then we both went our separate ways.

The next time that I remember seeing and talking with Larry was during one of the pro-Celebrity Golf tournaments that was held during DJ Convention time each year. He was in his golf cart and I believe they were playing Harpeth Hills Golf Course. Some of us had been following some celebrities around, watching them play golf, when Larry pulled up beside us and said "Hi." I walked over to his cart and talked for a few minutes with him. He then went off to play and we continued to follow whomever it was we were watching. I believe it was Mac Davis and his foursome.

Larry, I doubt very seriously if you would remember me today, as you have been very successful and we didn't really know each other that well, but I did know Dottie West, and she did know talent when she heard it - and you proved she was right!

RALPH EMERY ...

I don't know exactly when Ralph started with WSM radio doing the all-night *Ralph Emery Show,* but it was some time around late 1957 or early 1958. I believe he was doing that show when I first began working for Jim. It seems like I used to visit him on that show from the very beginning of my living in Nashville. I know when I first came to Nashville on a visit in March 1957, Smilin' Eddie Hill (who has since passed away) was doing the all-night show. I also know that Ralph and I have been friends for as long as I lived in *Music City,* and we still are, and we've shared many pleasant memories.

Every once in a while we have had the opportunity to recall some of those memories. Ralph and I were both at the funeral home during visitation when Dottie West was killed in that tragic car accident, and at that time he and I got to reminiscing about a lot of fun times where Dottie was involved and we called her *Beulah.* I told him that I had a copy of that list of nicknames and he asked if he could have a copy. The copy that I had was in pretty bad shape, so I typed it over and one night when I went to *Nashville Now* (the TNN TV show that Ralph hosted), with Mae Axton, I took him a copy. I went back to makeup where Ralph was having his hair done for the upcoming show and when I gave him the copy, he and I got into such a wonderful conversation and had all the girls in makeup listening to us reminiscing. Ralph stopped looking at the list and told all of them who I was and how we went back a long way.

About that time actress Florence Henderson (remember *The Brady Bunch* sitcom series?) came in and got rather caught up in our conversation, and our remembering when! Ralph introduced me to her. He told her that we'd been friends a long time, and about the list of nicknames. She thought it was great!

In 1991, Ralph thanks Joyce for appearing on his TNN show Nashville Now.

When Ralph first hosted the all-night radio show, it was in the old National Life Building at 7th and Union. WSM Radio and TV were then owned by that insurance company. I suppose that at one time or another, he had every artist as a guest on his show. That is where I first met many of them. I used to go up to his show a lot back then.

I recall when he and his wife Betty divorced (for the second time) and Ralph began dating Mattie George. Seems we were always at the same parties back then, and believe me there were many parties! Ralph and I were never more than just friends. However, he did ask me out a few times, but I never did go. As I told Ralph a few years ago, I was so afraid of him. I don't know why, as he had never been anything but nice to me, but I was. I remember he invited me to go to the Cotton Bowl and I turned him down, and he invited me to go to New York and I turned him down; then he asked me to go out and I said OK. Well, I called and cancelled the date that I'd made with him, telling him that my sister from Kentucky was in town. I lied, she wasn't visiting! I have always liked Ralph, but I could not help being afraid. I know he wouldn't believe that I had this fear of him, and Ralph, in one of your books you even wrote for me to never be afraid again. Sorry about the lie and I'm also sorry that I didn't keep that date.

The only time that I did go with Ralph was when Jim got killed and everyone had gone to Texas to attend his funeral. Ralph called and asked to take me to dinner and I went. It was the first time that I had ever eaten watermelon ice cream. He took me to the restaurant that was in The Continental Towers and was so sweet and nice to me. I'll always remember that evening. Makes me wonder why I was ever afraid to date him.

When they moved the radio station out to Knob Hill, I would still visit and sit up all night many times with Ralph and later with him and Tex Ritter. There were several times when Ralph interviewed me on the air about Jim. I remember one night when he had asked me to bring my collection of 78rpm recordings. We had such a good time playing them and commenting on the various artists. I had some 78's by Marty Robbins, Ray Price, Hank Williams, Sr., and of course most of Jim's old Abbott recordings.

It's hard to believe that so many years have passed since Studio A in the National Life Building. Ralph, you are now known all over the country because of the radio and TV personality that you have become, and also due to your best-selling books of your memories.

Everyone knows you in their own special way, but no one knows you in quite the same way that I do Ralph, and you know, even though I was afraid of you, I always loved you and still do. I'm proud of you and for you, and your many accomplishments and I'm proud of our friendship over the years, and all the good times. You also wrote in one of your books that some friendships are the forever kind and this is what ours is and I agree.

I thank you for staying the Ralph that I've always known and you can be assured that there has been at least one day out of each year since we've known each other that you are thought about by me, and I'd be willing to bet that you think about me on that day also. That date is March 10th, our mutual birthday.

When Ralph was the all-night DJ, artists always brought their new records by for him to review and play, as he sat in a powerful seat and could "make" a record. Below is a poem that I have written about this powerful all-night DJ.

THE ALL NIGHT DEEJAY
By Joyce Jackson, March 1994

HE WAS KNOWN TO MANY AS THE ALL-NIGHT DEEJAY
THEN LATER AS THE "NASHVILLE NOW" TV HOST
ARTISTS DROPPED BY WITH A RECORD IN HAND
OR WITH WHATEVER THEY WANTED TO PROMOTE

THEY WOULD TELL HIM HOW GREAT THEIR SONG WAS
AND WHY IT SHOULD MAKE THE TOP 10
IF THE SONG DIDN'T MAKE IT, THEY BLAMED IT ON HIM
FOR NOT GIVING THEIR RECORD ENOUGH SPINS

HE HAD THE POWER TO MAKE SONGS BECOME HITS
AND THE ARTISTS WERE WELL AWARE OF THIS, TOO
SO THEY'D BUTTER HIM UP AND PRETEND TO BE FRIEND
THEN BEHIND HIS BACK, OH THE TALKING THEY'D DO

HE'S RECEIVED MUCH ACCLAIM, THE WORLD KNOWS HIS NAME
BUT I'LL VENTURE WAY OUT ON A LIMB
THE WORLD OUT THERE MAY KNOW HIS NAME
BUT THEY'LL JUST NEVER KNOW THE REAL HIM

I DON'T KNOW ALL THAT THERE IS TO KNOW
BUT I PROBABLY KNOW A LOT MORE THAN MOST
AND THRE'S MUCH MORE TO THE RALPH THAT I KNOW
THAN JUST BEING A DEEJAY OR A TV SHOW HOST

TO ME HE'S SENSITIVE, KIND AND A FRIEND
AND I LOVE HIM IN MY OWN SPECIAL WAY
TO TOP OFF ALL THE THINGS THAT WE SHARE
WE ALSO CELEBRATE A MUTUAL BIRTHDAY

I LOVE YOU, RALPH, AND I ALWAYS WILL
IN YOUR WAY, I KNOW YOU LOVE ME, TOO
YOU'VE BEEN A GOOD FRIEND AND I TREASURE THAT
MAY GOD CONTINUE POURING BLESSINGS ON YOU

Ralph, you said you'd help me with this book and I'm gonna hold you to it!
Thanks for all the years of wonderful memories.

ROGER MILLER ...

What a magical year for me it was in 1958. It was the beginning of my establishing friendships with so many that are now "greats" in this industry called music. I thank Heaven that Roger Miller was one of those "greats" that I was able to call my friend.

I have written so much about Roger in other segments of this book. So much so, that very little else needs to be written, except that I feel the world lost one of its better talents when Roger died Oct. 25, 1992, at age 56. He was certainly a multi-talented individual and in my opinion, had just begun to truly uncover his vast talent.

Jim recorded several Roger Miller songs, such as "Home," "Billy Bayou," "If Heartache Is The Fashion," "When Two Worlds Collide" and one of my favorites that Jim only did in an album, titled "I Catch Myself Crying." I don't think RCA ever put this out as a single, but they should have, as it is a beautiful song.

The last time that I saw Roger in person was several years ago at the Stockyard Restaurant's Bullpen Lounge in Nashville. A group of us had gone there to listen to the band and I saw Roger sitting across the room. It had been a long time since I had seem him, as he had moved to New Mexico. I went over and we had such a good time talking and doing some remembering. He had his wife Mary (she was his third wife) with him and he introduced me to her and said to Mary, "Do you remember when we were having dinner the other night out and I told you that the waitress that served us looked just like someone that I know back in Nashville? Well, this is the girl that I know back in Nashville."

Roger had the quickest, wittiest, and the most delightful comeback answers of anyone that I know and whenever you were around him, you couldn't help but laugh. To me, Roger was the one person that could put you on a natural high!

I knew the Roger of the earlier years and unfortunately didn't have an opportunity to be around Roger much after he and Barbara, his first wife, divorced and he moved to California and remarried. Leah was his second wife and he was married to her the year that he won six Grammies (for 1965) awarded in 1966. I was fortunate enough to have been at that particular Grammy show when my date was Lionel Delmore, son of Alton Delmore, of the vintage country duet The Delmore Brothers (with brother Rabon). I was so happy and proud of Roger as he deserved every award that he received. The year before (1964), he had won five Grammys.

Roger was one of the cleverest songwriters and was forever being copied. He also wrote some of the most beautiful songs, such as "The Last Word In Lonesome Is Me." a melodic, yet cleverly written number that he did so well. Who will forget songs like "Dang Me," "You Can't Roller Skate In A Buffalo Herd," "England Swings" and, of course, "King Of The Road." These were songs Roger made up to sing at parties and fun get-togethers. I heard them at least two years before they were released. He'd sing them at Charlie Dick's or at Dottie West's house, when we'd all be there partying.

I could write page after page, singing Roger's praises about one song or another that he's written, making him the well-known writer that he was. But I'd prefer you, who have not been fortunate enough to know or be acquainted with his talents, take a little time and seek out his work and really listen to this truly talented man.

Roger, I believe that your work had just begun and now what a publisher you have to write for! God, I am glad that I knew you as a friend. You were special while here on earth, but now you're even more special because of whose company you're in.

I know that you know, that many people loved you and they still miss you. Each of our lives were made better simply because we had the wonderful opportunity of knowing you, Roger. But you couldn't possibly know just how many people you touched in one way or another. I know that I'm so thankful that I've known you. Roger, I also want you to know that I have always tried to be the lady that you told me you felt I was. Thank you for that comment. It has always been my secret treasure, knowing you felt that way about me. You were truly one of a kind, a unique, talented human being. Your leaving left a void in our business, and I know they all miss you, as I do. You were such a special person and friend. (Roger was posthumously inducted into the Country Music Hall of Fame in 1995.)

Roger Miller

Songwriter Lionel Delmore escorted Joyce to the '66 Grammy show when Roger received multiple awards.

MEL TILLIS ...

Mel came to Nashville a little earlier than I did, primarily scoring as a songwriter initially. I know that I met him right after I arrived. Again, it was down at Linebaugh's when he came in with Wayne Walker, another writer. Wayne had already become an established writer, having had Andy Williams' hit with his song "Are You Sincere." He and Mel were great friends and wrote songs together back then. Wayne married Elaine Tubb (Ernest's daughter) about this same time.

Being a songwriter first helped Mel get established as a recording artist. Now Mel will be remembered as not only a wonderful songwriter, but as a great entertainer, as well. Don't miss his show should you get the chance. You will be entertained.

When we had our promotion office in the RCA Building - and even before - I would take songs to Mel to listen to from time-to-time, with the hope that he would record one. Finally, he found one that he liked well enough to cut. It was a Buddy Mize song (Buddy wrote for Acclaim Music, one of our publishing companies that Jim founded). It was a song titled "Somebody's Puttin' Somebody On." I was so happy that Mel recorded it, because that song established me as a "songplugger."

I always had such a good time when I would stop by Mel's office. He was a very good business man and I told him that he reminded me a great deal of Jim in how he handled business. We had many good conversations there in his office after office hours. I remember one night I had stopped in around closing time, when he had his office on 18th and West End Avenue. He and I had a drink and talked and had more drinks and talked, and I don't remember too much about that visit, except that I fell asleep on his office floor (don't ask me what I was doing on the floor, 'cause I don't know). He evidently fell asleep also. I remember waking up and it was in the wee hours of the morning and I know I left because I got home, but all of that's very foggy to me. I was wondering if you remember anything about that particular night, Mel?

Mel was also one of the people that would join us to play softball on Sunday's at Edwin Warner Park. We all had such a good time being together and sharing each other's families, and I know now that it was God blessing each of us and we just didn't realize it at the time. The reason I know it was God blessing us, is because it was something so very special and it still is today, and all good and perfect gifts come from Him. Those times were just perfect.

I remember one night when a group of us had gone to Ralph Emery's all-night radio

show and Mel was one of his guests. He was there plugging a new record. Ralph asked him if his speech handicap (Mel stuttered) was a hindrance to his singing career and Mel said, *"No, Ralph, it's been an ass . ., ass . ., ass . ., asset to my career."* Mel was always such a good sport when we'd laugh at his stammering. I feel it was because he knew in his heart that we were laughing *with* him and not *at* him, and God turned his handicap into a tool to move Mel up the success ladder and now he enjoys having the last laugh!

When I went to Branson to work in the Willie Nelson Museum and Theater in 1992, I ran into Mel at one of the restaurants there, and he made me feel as though he truly was glad to see me again. It had been quite some time since our last meeting. At that time he also had a club there called The Mole Hole, which he later sold.

Thanks for always treating me the same, no matter where it is that I see you. I don't think you have ever failed to ask about my daughter - and that is so special to me, as it always made me feel that you did genuinely care about me.

Mel was another one that was always there when I would call on him, whether it was for a donation for a charity that I was involved with, or whether it was as a sponsor for our local Bass 'N Gal Fishing Club. He was all for the club, as he also enjoyed fishing very much.

Mel, I personally feel that you are one of the best entertainers that this industry has

My Memories ...

ever, or will ever, produce - and I thank God for allowing our paths to cross - and a friendship to be established.

Just this year, March 2009, Mel played in Colorado Springs, and I had the pleasure of meeting and visiting with him on his bus, catching up on some old memories.. What fun it was seeing him again. He even got me a ticket to the show and what a great show he and his Statesiders put on!

Here is a copy of the ticket to his show here in Colorado Springs, plus a photo of he and I on his bus.

Mel used to call me "Super Squirrel" and he was "Gus." In another photo included, he is "Gus." As you can see, he signed it to "Super Squirrel."

I love ya M-M-M-Mel!

This shot was captured aboard Mel's tour bus.

FLOYD CRAMER ...

Pianist Floyd Cramer was one of the original A Team musicians who helped fashion the fabled *Nashville Sound.* I met Floyd after I started working for Jim, as he was playing piano for him on the *Grand Ole Opry*, and its *Friday Night Frolics,* as well as on Jim's recording sessions. In fact, Floyd can be heard on most of Jim's recordings. He had also been a member of Jim's band called The Wagonmasters, before Jim relinquished that title to Porter Wagoner, and renamed his band the Blue Boys, after one of his hit singles.

You won't find a nicer person around than Floyd. I loved Floyd and his wife Mary very much, and like so many of the other legends or greats in the music industry, I just took them for granted, as I was around him a great deal and he was my friend and his office was just across the hall from mine. I even helped him answer his fan mail.

Sometimes I forget just how much these people have contributed to this industry and how our particular style of music has grown to what it is today. It's people like Floyd, Jim, Chet, Owen, Eddy, Marty, Ernest . . . and the list goes on and on . . . that laid the groundwork for today. Unfortunately, not many of our artists today give thanks for what these people did to open the doors for them. There was a time when country music wasn't accepted in all homes, as it is now, but thanks to these wonderful legends and many others like them that bridged the gap from then to now, our music is finally accepted.

Floyd, in my opinion, was a vital part of bridging that gap, when he became an artist in his own right, rather than being just a musician who backed up other artists. Who can forget his #1 instrumental country-pop crossover single "Last Date," one of his own compositions that sold over a million copies. It was such a beautiful, yet simple song and was recorded by about every instrumentalist that had a recording contract. Skeeter Davis even put lyrics to it (collaborating with Boudleaux Bryant), retitling it "My Last Date (With You)," recorded it, and it also became a big hit for her! Conway Twitty did the same thing a dozen years later, rewriting the lyrics, retitled it, and enjoyed a #1 record with "(Lost Her Love) On Our Last Date."

When I had my office across the hall from Floyd, one day when my daughter Joy was about 7 years old, I had her with me at the office, so we went over to visit with him. She and Floyd sat at Floyd's piano and played a duet together. They played "Mary Had A Little Lamb." Joy was just learning how to play the piano and she was so impressed with him, and I'll never forget how sweet he was to take the time he did with her.

Later, after she was out of school and had joined the Navy, she was stationed in San Diego and Floyd had a TV double album out and had advertising spots on most of the TV stations. She told various ones that she knew him when she'd see that advertisement, and that she and Floyd had even played a duet together at one time. Of course, no one believed her, but once when she came home on leave - not long after the album was out - we went to see Floyd and Mary and when she told Floyd that her friends didn't believe her when she told them she knew him or that they had played a duet together, he got up and went into another room and came back with a set of tapes for her and me, but on one of hers he wrote, "To Joy, let's play another duet together, Love Floyd." He wanted her to take it back and show the others that she did know him and that they had done what she told them she had. That was just the kind of person Floyd was.

When the Opry was still in the Ryman Auditorium (the Opry moved to its new location at Opryland in 1974), back in the late 1950's and early 1960's, Floyd was more or less the staff pianist, and when he'd have a break between shows, he'd be down at Linebaugh's playing the pinball machine. After the Opry was over, he'd be back at that pinball machine for a little while, then he'd be out and gone. He was never one to sit up all night, like so many of us did down at that restaurant.

To help put Joy through school, I started baking cakes. I made all kinds of birthday cakes and wedding and anniversary cakes. It was a pretty good side business and really helped me out. Floyd and Mary were two of my best customers. They and their daughters all ordered cakes from me. I appreciated that then and still do.

Floyd Cramer and Joyce.

Floyd has always been one of my very favorite people in or out of our business. I treasure the years of friendship that I had the opportunity to share with him. Even though he was a legend - and he was - he never changed, and that's what helped make him a legend. I sure did love ya, Floyd, and you, too, Mary. We'll share lunch again one of these days, OK?

Their grandson, Jason Floyd Coleman, has followed in his Grandfather's footsteps and has become a very accomplished pianist. For Christmas 2007, Mary sent me a copy of Jason's CD titled "Faith." It is just beautiful and it sure brought tears to my eyes, as I was imagining Floyd looking down and being so proud. Thank you, Mary. I also remember when Jason was born. Floyd gave out golf balls announcing his birth. I still have mine. Floyd went home to be with the Lord, Dec. 31, 1997.

JIMMY WAKELY ...

Many of you may not even remember who Jimmy Wakely was, but by the same token, many will. I met Jimmy at a radio station in Louisville, somewhere around 1953 or 1954. I knew he was going to be there and so I made it a point to be at that station, as I was a big fan of his. I still am today, but you just never hear anything about him any more. I loved his duets with Margaret Whiting, and one of my favorites is "Slipping Around." (He also did some splendid solo recordings, including "One Has My Name.")

I wish I had taken a photo of he and I together back then, but I didn't and the only thing I have is an autograph on the back of someone's business card and the memory of how nice and sweet he was. He was so kind and one thing that stands out most about him was his wonderful smile, and he smiled a great deal.

Jimmy, I know you will never read this book, but hopefully someone in your family just might and in case they do, I want them to know just how very special my memory of you is, and it has always remained in my heart and mind all these many years. Not only were you kind and sweet, but you were so darnned good looking!

I'm so happy to have had the opportunity to meet you. (Jimmy, who also made his mark in Hollywood Westerns, died Sept. 23, 1982, at age 68.)

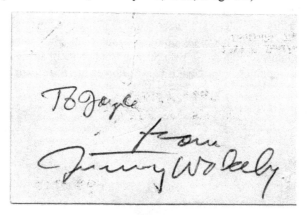

JIM ED BROWN ...

I met all of The Browns, Jim Ed, Maxine and Bonnie, the day that Jim hired me. They were in town to record and stopped by Jim's office to visit awhile with him. I got to know Jim Ed and Maxine better than I did Bonnie, as both of them moved to Nashville, whereas Bonnie stayed in Arkansas. They were from Pine Bluff, Ark. They have another sister, Norma, but I only met her a couple of times and really didn't get to know her at all.

Jim Ed and I had a couple of dates when he would come to Nashville, but basically we were just friends. Later, he married Becky and she also became my friend. Not many people know that Jim played rhythm on many of The Browns' sessions, because they liked the sound he gave them, and they were also very good friends of him and Mary. Like Jim, The Browns were initially recorded by Fabor Robinson (on his subsidiary label Fabor Records), before being signed by RCA.

When Frank and Jeanie Oakley and I were gathering items for The Willie Nelson & Friends Museum, we went to Jim Ed and he lent us one of his stage suits and a form to display it on. He was also present when we had our Grand Opening at The Jim Reeves Museum and for our special Texas Day at the museum.

I have always thought a great deal of Jim Ed and his pet name for me was "Tiger," but I have to say that I was somewhat disappointed when I found out that he had become involved with Ed Gregory, as some kind of business partner, but I don't know to just what extent, back when Gregory bought all of the Jim Reeves Enterprises' business with a non-secured note. (Ed Gregory has since died.)

This sale devastated Mary, along with those of us who loved her. She once told me, "They are taking everything away from me." I know that Tom Perryman was also in on negotiations for the sale, and I know that they thought at the time that they were doing Mary a favor I guess, but in my opinion, it only caused her illness to worsen.

Jim Ed, I've known you now for over 50 years and you will always have a special place in my heart, and yes, I am thankful God allowed my life's path to cross your's and your sisters'.

Jim Ed and Joy Jackson, Joyce's daughter.

JOHNNY DUNCAN ...

When I first met Johnny Duncan, he was playing the Town Towers Motel Lounge in Bowling Green, Ky., in 1966. Mary Reeves and I went up to hear him one night. Mary had met him before and thought he was a very good talent. We had such a good time, but then I always had a good time with Mary. Johnny came to our table during one of his breaks, and Mary introduced him to me. I remember thinking that this was one good looking man! And he sure did have a lot of talent.

After that, Johnny would always come by and visit us in our hospitality suites each year during the DJ Conventions, and he was always so nice. We would get into some great conversations during those visits. I just loved him and thought he was about the sexiest man in the whole music industry. I used to tell him that all the time, but I don't think he ever took me seriously, but I meant every word.

Johnny enjoyed a few hit recordings (like "It Couldn't Have Been Any Better" and "She Can Put Her Shoes Under My Bed (Anytime)"), but I don't feel he ever achieved the superstar status that he deserved. He had some hit duets with Janie Fricke, too, such as "Stranger" and an early hit by himself titled "Sweet Country Woman" and enjoyed some TV exposure, but he just never got the right kind of recognition. (He was a cousin to talented Brady, Dan and Troy Seals.)

The last time I saw Johnny was during Fan Fair 1989. I was working in the Willie Nelson booth and he came over and visited. We had a great conversation and I remember telling him again how much I had always thought of him and his talent, and I still think that he was the sexiest man in the music industry - and one of the nicest. He was definitely no "stranger" to me. Johnny died Aug. 14, 2006, at age 67. He is missed!

CHARLEY PRIDE ...

It was in the mid-1960's when I first met Charley Pride. I know that we were all upstairs in the back room at Tootsie's Orchid Lounge in downtown Nashville. Mary Reeves and most of The Blue Boys, along with Darla Kent Dorris, Ginny King and me, were all down there for some reason or another, probably just because Mary wanted us all with her. At any rate, Charley came up and joined us at our table. He knew Mary, as Jim had been a very influential artist to him and his musical career. We talked for a long time with him and I remember that he had just come back from New York and was telling us that he had been interviewed by *Time* magazine. His story never got printed, however, because the interviewer kept trying to bring racism into the interview and insisting that he was sure Charley was involved with some racial outfit, such as SNICK or the NAACP or some organization of this nature. Charley laughed and told us that he told the interviewer that the only organizations that he belonged to were the First Baptist Church and the CMA, and that stood for Country Music Association! Apparently, the man from *Time* just gave up and did not give Charley a story,.

Without *Time's* help, this innovative artist attained 29 #1 *Billboard* hits, including "Kiss An Angel Good Morning" and "Never Been So Loved (In All Of My Life)." I used to see Charley down at RCA's Studio B before the *new* building (which is now the old building) was built on Music Row. We'd sit in the reception room and have some good ol' talks. That's when I found out that his birthday was March 18th. Mine is March 10, and we started calling each other "fish" when we'd see each other after that. (According to the horoscope, those born under sign of the Fish - Pisces - are traditionally imaginative, sensitive, compassionate, selfless and unworldly.)

Charley and his wife Rosine always came by our suites during the DJ Conventions to say *Hi* to Mary and visit with all of us. They were so nice and we always enjoyed them coming by. I remember one time that Rosine and some of the executives from RCA in New York and I, all went to The Chicken Shack. We had to sit in the back! We both got a kick out of that!

There was a Robert Altman movie out in 1975 simply called "Nashville," which starred Lily Tomlin, Henry Gibson, Karen Black , Keith Carradine, Ronee Blakely and I don't recall who all else, but one of the scenes was shot at The Parthenon in Nashville's Centennial Park, and my brother-in-law Stu was part of the band. (He plays pedal steel guitar.) They needed some people to gather around the bandstand, so his wife Marsha, their two girls and me and my daughter Joy, all went to be part of the crowd scene. The camera focused in on us about three different times, while filming that particular scene. It wasn't long after the movie came out when it was Convention time again and I was sitting just outside the RCA Suite when Charley came by and told me that he'd seen me in "Nashville" and I asked what he was talking about, as, of course, we were in Nashville. He laughed and then said *the movie* "Nashville."

Charley, it goes without question that you are the very first black superstar in the country music firmament, and you are so respected by all who have been fortunate enough to have met you. I know that I am honored that our paths crossed on many different occasions, and that you were inducted into the Country Music Hall of Fame in 2000.

I thank you "Fish" for some very pleasant memories, and for your contributions to our industry with so many great songs and especially for your album tribute to Jim.

Charley greets Joyce backstage.

STEVE WARINER ...

When Ralph Emery had a press conference for one of his books ("More Memories . . ."), which I believe was in early 1995. I was invited and this is where I first saw Steve Wariner. Chet Atkins had brought him to the event, as he was a great guitarist and was a prodigy of Chet's, even though he was actually discovered by Dottie West.

By the time of the press conference, Steve had already amassed nine #1 records. Anyway, I had wanted to meet him because he was a favorite of both my daughter Joy and her husband when they were dating. Chet introduced me to Steve and I told him abut how Joy and her then-husband Dennis loved his music, and how they had dated listening to his records when both were stationed in Sinop, Turkey. Being both in the Navy, Steve's recordings made them feel closer to home.

Steve seemed very happy to hear about this and said no one had ever said that about his music before, and asked where they lived and when I told him in Colorado Springs, Colo., he said that in about three weeks he would be playing The Grizzly Rose in Denver, and asked if they would come and be his special guests for the night. I assured him they would be delighted, as they were about to celebrate their anniversary and how special his concert would be for them. I called and, of course, they were very happy. Steve asked me to call his office the next day to get it all arranged.

I called and talked with his wife Caryn and she said she would have tickets waiting at the box office window. Everyone followed through and sure enough the tickets were waiting for them and a table was reserved right up front for Joy, and she said Steve could not have been nicer. He had backstage passes for them as well, and during one of the breaks he joined their table and they discussed how much both of them loved Dottie and just talked in general.

They did go backstage, but only to say goodbye and thank Steve for being so gracious, and to tell him how much they appreciated him and his music.

Even though I only met Steve that one time, I felt this sweet story needed to be shared to show what a great guy he is. He not only is a great guitarist, but a terrific singer as well. His records - including "All Roads Lead To You" and "Life's Highway"- are so easy to listen to, and Steve, I know I thanked you when we talked that night, and believe I even sent a little *thank you* note, but you will never know just how special you made two people feel. So, again I thank you for doing what you said you would do, and for being so nice to two people that mean so much to me.

Joy, the author's daughter, with Steve
Wariner and Joy's former husband Dennis.

DOLLY PARTON ...

Dolly first came to Nashville in June 1964, but I didn't meet her until some time later. Among her first hit recordings were Top 10 duets with Bill Phillips ("Put It Off Until Tomorrow" and "The Company You Keep," which she co-wrote) and one of her earliest solo recordings was "Dumb Blonde" and how true that song was. There is a line that says, *"This dumb blonde ain't nobody's fool."* There isn't anyone that can say that Dolly is anybody's fool. She's proven herself time and time again that she can sing, write great songs, act, and truly entertain.

The one thing that I love about Dolly is her attitude of what you see is what you get! She has always been the same, whether it was on *The Johnny Carson Tonight Show,* doing her own show, or meeting her in the halls of the RCA Building. That's where I got to know Dolly pretty good. She recorded for RCA and having my office there, I would run into her quite frequently. She knew who I was and was always very friendly when we'd meet. She had this little giggle that I know all have heard on TV.

When Dolly was elected to the Country Music Hall of Fame in 1999, she was to do a show at the old Country Music Hall of Fame building. I was invited to that show, as were Jim's nieces Lani Arnold, Kay and Carolyn. We all went together and talked with Dolly briefly. I told her that I knew she didn't remember me, but that we used to see each other in the halls of RCA all the time and kinda laughed. She said, "Well, I wouldn't have remembered you until you laughed, but yes, I do." I said, "Dolly, you wouldn't put me on would you?" She said, "Yes, I would, but I'm not." I then told her that I was Stu Basore's sister-in-law and she squealed and said for me to tell Stu hi for her. Stu played steel guitar on Dolly's earlier RCA hits such as "Jolene," "Love is Like A Butterfly" and "I Will Always Love You," to name a few. She was so cute and did a terrific show. I haven't seen Dolly since that night in 1999, except on TV and in some of the rag magazines. I wish they would leave her alone!

Dolly and Carol Burnett did a show at the Grand Ole Opry House some years ago and I was fortunate enough to catch that show. When you left, you had truly been entertained! These two in my opinion, are about the greatest female entertainers around or ever will be for that matter. They were so different, yet blended so well.

Love you for always being just Dolly, no matter where your stage is. You are truly one in a million, and I am so honored that our paths crossed as much or as little as they did. You are indeed a special lady!

Dolly Parton on the red carpet.

Dolly, incidentally, appeared in a number of movies, including "9 To 5," for which her title tune was Oscar nominated, "Best Little Whorehouse in Texas," "Steel Magnolias" and "Straight Talk." Further, the superstar's "9 To 5" spun off into a TV sitcom series and finally a Broadway show. Like Jim Reeves, she is an equally popular artist abroad.

ELVIS PRESLEY ...

There's not a great deal that I can personally tell about Elvis Presley, as I'm sorry to say that he's one legend that I did not know. Like millions of others, however, I feel like I did, as I was able to watch him grow in his successes. I only went to one concert, which was great, but being given the opportunity to meet and see him up close I suppose, was one of the most exciting times of my being involved with the music industry.

It was in back of the RCA studios in 1973. I was good friends with Vicky Mabe Vaughn. Vicky was Wally Cochran's secretary and Wally was the promotion director for RCA then, and she knew that Elvis was going to be recording on this particular day. She told me to go home and get Joy and she would go get her kids and we would wait for him in the back parking lot. We did that and I'll never forget the thrill it was seeing him pull up and get out of his limo. He nodded, then asked us how we were doing. I don't think any of us said anything. I know that we didn't run up to him or bother him in any way, and that was the extent of our meeting with him.

Elvis went in to record and we went home, taking with us a beautiful memory that I have cherished for so many years. It was wonderful being able to see him face-to-face and up close. He was so handsome and seemed so very nice. He didn't get all bent out of shape because we were there. He was just polite and courteous. There will never be another like him in my opinion, that will have the impact on the music industry that

Elvis did and I'm just thankful that my life was touched by him. He gave so much in such a short lifetime.

I really missed my big opportunity to visit Elvis in 1957, when I was visiting Nashville. Gordon Terry (one of the industry's greatest fiddle players) offered to take me to see him. Another girl was also visiting from Minnesota by the name of Sharon Begin Lange. Gordon was going to take us both down to Memphis. I declined, as I had promised Shirley Valliere (Faron Young's secretary) that I would help her with Faron's fan club journal or some such thing. Sharon went and they had a wonderful visit with Elvis. Gordon and he were friends. I have kicked myself a thousand times for not going, but at least I kept my promise to Shirley and I guess Faron was worth it. I must have thought so back then.

Elvis, if it were possible for me to tell you today how I feel about you, I would like to say that I appreciate the fact that you loved your mother so much, and I thank you for giving us so much of yourself through music, and I thank my God our paths did cross even for that brief moment in back of the RCA studios . . . You were king here in the music world, but you're now with the King of Kings. (Elvis died Aug. 16, 1977, at age 42).

PORTER WAGONER ...

I first met Porter Wagoner backstage at the *Grand Ole Opry* in the Ryman Auditorium when I came to Nashville in January 1958. He told me then that he had only been there a few months before I came. I have always been impressed with the fact that Porter seemed to see the funny side of life and its situations. I'm sure that is not always true, but he made it appear so.

You could also be assured of hearing at least half a dozen jokes whenever you talked with him. Porter and Don Helms (Don was one of the original Drifting Cowboys, Hank Williams' band) are my two favorite joke tellers. They have such fun with them that you can't help enjoying them.

Now Porter loved to fish and so do I. When I became a member of the Bass 'N Gal Association, our Music City Bass 'N Gal affiliate club held a national tournament on Nashville's Percy Priest Lake. Our club had to have in escrow a purse of $1,000 before the national club would hold a tournament in Nashville. There is a lot involved when you host a fishing tournament, but I was selected to obtain our sponsors to put up the money needed in escrow. I assured our members that I knew enough people in our music industry that loved to fish that could help us out. I had enough faith in my friendships with these people that I knew I could call on them.

Porter was one of the first ones I called on. Our idea was to have 10 sponsors and ask for $100 each. I remember the day I went into Porter's office and told him my story. He thought it was a great thing that a group of girls enjoyed a sport that he also loved and without any hesitation whatsoever, he just reached into his pocket and pulled out a hundred dollar bill and gave it to me. I was expecting a check, so I had to mail him his receipt!

When I used to pitch songs for our publishing companies that were a part of Jim Reeves Enterprises, Porter never refused to see me. He never did record any of the songs that I pitched him, but he did listen to what I would bring him.

I remember one day when we were in his office listening to material, and in waltzed Dolly Parton just a giggling like she does any time you see her. She was so cute. She is in person just like you see her on TV. I love that about her.

Porter's been linked with first one girl singer and another, and I've heard all kinds of different stories about him and women, but I remember one time during one of the DJ Conventions when I had had a little too much to drink and I got to talking with Porter in the RCA Suite and invited him to go to my room with me. He came, but was a perfect gentleman and even found me some coffee and told me that he could not and would not take advantage of me, and he never ever mentioned that time to me again, but always stayed just as friendly as ever. I don't think I ever thanked him for the way he treated me, but I am very thankful and most grateful.

My brother-in-law Stu traveled with Porter on the road for quite some time and was also a part of Porter's TV show, especially when he did it from Opryland Park. Actually, I was never really around Porter too much, other than when I would see and talk with him backstage at the Opry, so I personally didn't know too much about him.

Except that he was always good to me and a perfect gentleman, also fun to be around and one heck of a nice guy. Porter died Oct. 28, 2007, at age 80.

Joyce and Porter.

Porter with Joyce's sis Jan Beaverson.

MERLE KILGORE ...

Merle Kilgore was in town for a DJ Convention, escorting Billie Jean Horton (Johnny Horton's widow) around, when I first met him They had been friends for quite some time, and this was before he moved here.

Merle and I became friends a long time ago, and he was on the same show in Louisville as the Wilburn Brothers when I went with them. During one of our conversations, I told Merle that I was from Pewee Valley and that he should write a song about it, as it was a sweet little town. Merle had written the big hit "Wolverton Mountain" recorded by Claude King, and even though Merle had written many songs by then (including Webb Pierce's #1 "More and More"), this one really put him on the map as an established songwriter.

It wasn't too long after our conversation in Louisville, that I ran into him and he told me he had written the song "Pewee Valley," about this little girl from there that had a great big love. He said he had patterned the little girl after me and that pop singer Vaughn Monroe was coming out with that song. Vaughn did come out with it, but it never got to be a hit recording, even though I thought it was good; but remember, it was about this little town that I'm from in Kentucky. Every time after that, whenever I'd run into Merle, he'd start singing that song for me.

Merle was a wonderful promoter and I personally feel that he is responsible for the success that Hank Williams, Jr., has attained. At the time of Merle's death on Feb. 6, 2005, at 70, he was the manager of Hank, Jr. He is missed by those in all phases of the music industry and I will miss my friend.

Merle and Joyce, above; and that's Merle (left) in the photo at right with Jim Lawrence, Bill Rains and Charlie Dick, at the unveilings of Rains' sculptures of Hank Snow, Buck Owens and Johnny Cash in Nashville.

RONNIE MILSAP ...

There are some that I know or knew quite well, but we didn't run with the same crowd and therefore there isn't much of a story to tell about them. Ronnie is one of those who comes to mind in this way. Ronnie is such a talented singer and a great guy. He is blind and has been since birth, but he is so awesome. I told him one time when we met in the hall at RCA that my first job was printing Braille books and that I had worked with the blind, partially blind and with mutes, and it was quite an education, and that one of the main things that I learned was that the blind are only as handicapped as we make them. He told me he wished everyone knew that.

Ronnie used to have a night that he called "Lost in the Fifties" (after one of his songs by that title) once a year, and Carolyn Sells and I would go together. It was always such a good time and also fun to listen to the oldies of yesteryear. Ronnie has enjoyed many hit recordings and he also did a tribute album to Jim. His hits include songs like "Daydreams About Night Things," "It Was Almost Like a Song," "I Wouldn't Have

Missed It For The World" and one of my very favorites is "Smoky Mountain Rain." Ronnie is another one that should wear a white hat, as he is truly one of the good guys.

JOHNNY BOND ...

Johnny was one of Gene Autry's sidekicks on their radio program back in the 1940's. I used to listen to it all the time. I was just a little kid then, but I loved that program. It was called *Melody Ranch* starring Gene Autry and the Melody Ranch Boys. They always told a good story and Johnny was one o the boys. It was around 1963, when Jim cut a song that was in Johnny's publishing company and he came out to our office. I remember how thrilled I was to meet one of Gene Autry's sidekicks from so many years ago. He was such a gentleman and Jim was the one who introduced me to him and I don't remember what I even said to him, as I was awestruck. I just couldn't believe that I was meeting this man that I had listened to so many years before and had enjoyed so much. I have been a fan of many artists, but this man was just so special. I truly thank God that he allowed our paths to cross. Johnny was a fine writer and recording star in his own right, with hits like "Divorce Me C.O.D." and "10 Little Bottles."Johnny died June 12, 1978 at 63, but posthumously was inducted into the Country Music Hall of Fame in 1999. Another hit of his I recall was "So Round, So Firm, So Fully Packed." Hope some of you will also remember that one and maybe it will bring a smile, as it just did to me.

JOHNNY HORTON ...

I only met him one time and I wasn't too happy with him at that time either. As I have said before, Billy Graves and I met the very first night that I was in Nashville when I moved here and he was one half of The Country Lads that were regulars on *The Jimmy Dean Show.* They were in town to record and Billy had called me and I went to his hotel room where he was listening to various songwriters' material that they were pitching with the hope for recordings. Most everyone had left and I thought I would be able to spend a little time with Billy, whom I liked very much, when Johnny knocked on the door and brought several songs which Billy listened to, then he continued to stay and stay . . . and talked and talked, until it was getting too late for me to stay any longer, so I bid goodbye to Billy, with Johnny still there in the room. Although my memory of Johnny wasn't a pleasurable one, I did enjoy his recordings, some very big hits such as "Honky Tonk Man," "The Battle of New Orleans," "Johnny Reb" and "North To Alaska." Johnny was killed in an automobile crash Nov. 5, 1960 (age 35), not too long after I'd met him. It was announced during the RCA Breakfast at the 1960 convention. Although I wasn't happy about it then, I am glad we met.

TANYA TUCKER ...

Tanya is another one that I only met a few times. I initially met her when Willie Nelson and Hank Cochran formed their publishing company Co-Heart Music and had a grand opening. Tanya came and brought her daughter Presley Tanita with her. I introduced myself to her and she was polite, but I did not feel she was very friendly and would rather that I had not even spoken to her.

Mae Axton was a very good friend of mine and she was also a friend of Tanya's and was in fact the Godmother of Tanita. Mae asked me to make the cake for Tanita's Christening, which I did and this was what I told Tanya, so she would know that I wasn't just a nutty fan trying to make conversation. Perhaps she just wasn't feeling well on this particular night. Artists have their off nights, too! It really doesn't matter because I understand that a person can't be "on" all of the time.

Regardless of how Tanya treated me that night, I still feel that she is one of the most talented female artists that our industry has ever shared with the public, and feel that she was long overlooked when it came to giving out awards for accomplishments.

I thank Mae for asking me to make the cake for such a memorable time in Tanita's life. Being a friend of Mae Axton's convinces me that Tanya is really an OK person and Tanya, I wish you continued success in your career and in your personal life. God bless you now and always.

BRENDA LEE ...

What a great talent she is, and I had the pleasure of meeting and getting to know her a little. Lee Rosenberg, who helped launch Johnny Tillotson's career, is the one who introduced me to Brenda back in 1958, not long after I relocated here. I had an apartment across the street from Lee's house and she asked me over, and Brenda and her mother Grace were there. She was only 13 at that time, and already an established artist with recordings and national TV appearances under her tiny belt. One thing that has always impressed me about Brenda is her "I know what I want in a song" attitude. I remember going to one of her recording sessions and here was this little girl telling the musicians just how she wanted them to play on a song she was about to record. She had hit after hit, under the very capable direction of Owen Bradley, one of Nashville's pioneers of

Joyce and Brenda.

the *Nashville Sound* and head of Decca Records' country division.

Brenda always remembered me whenever we met. She became fairly good friends with my sister, Glenda, back when Glenda was taking care of Doyle and Margie Wilburn's daughter Sharon. Brenda was always a lot of fun to be around and really quite funny. She had her own style of "country humor."

I have followed her career from hit recording artist to wife to Mom and back to hit recording artist. Her talents are varied and she's a pro at each of them. With good reason, she's called *Little Miss Dynamite!*

I don't remember how many seasons that she performed at Opryland, but I hope if any of you were in Nashville during that particular time that you did catch her show in the Roy Acuff Theater, because if you did, you had the opportunity to see her versatility in person! It has always amazed me that such volume can come from such a small person.

I had the opportunity to see and visit again with Brenda when we both attended the toast to BMI's Frances Preston, where Brenda was an emcee. She is just as good at talking as she is at performing! I love her honesty as a person and as an entertainer ... She is a class act and I'm proud that we can have a fun conversation now and then. Love your singing, Brenda. (She is a member of both the Rock& Roll Hall of Fame and the Country Music Hall of Fame.)

GRANDPA JONES ...

Grandpa was just a jewel of a person, but he is another one that I didn't know very well. We were in Alabama one time - and I hate it, but I can't remember who I went down there with - but Grandpa went with us to get something to eat and he did a comedic drawing on a napkin of a man, and gave it to me. It has faded so now that I know it would not show up, but it is so cute and I just loved talking with him. Song- wise, I suppose Grandpa's biggest hit was "Eight More Miles To Louisville" (and he scored a Top Five with "T For Texas" in 1962). Grandpa was elected to the Country Music Hall of Fame in 1978.

Jean Shepard, Grandpa and Joyce.

Grandpa was a regular on the TV show *Hee Haw.* Loved that show and its down-to-earth humor.He also played in their band along with the likes of Roy Clark, Buck Trent, Chet Atkins and Floyd Cramer. I think everyone loved to appear on *Hee Haw,* and most of the artists of that era did so at one time or another, including his fiddler wife Ramona. Another regular was Stringbean (David Akeman). I loved him, too, and ran into him at Sears, just about a week before he and his wife were murdered. We had quite a conversation in Men's-wear. What a tragedy it was when we lost him. Grandpa passed away Feb. 19, 1998. Stringbean and his wife Estelle were both murdered on Nov. 11, 1973. As of this writing, his murderers are still in prison, I believe.

HOYT AXTON ...

There is no way you can be friends for as many years as I was with Mae Axton and not also get to know her son Hoyt! I've seen Hoyt many times over the years, when he would be visiting Mae or when he was in town to do some of the Nashville-based TV shows or to record.

Hoyt was also on the show that performed in Montana, when Mae and I were there for their Centennial Cattle Drive in September 1989.

Once when Hoyt was in Nashville to appear on TNN's *Crook & Chase,* I was out at Mae's and while we were waiting for Hoyt to get back to the house, time kinda got away from us and all of a sudden Mae said it was time for Hoyt and she hadn't pre-

Mama Mae and actor-singer-songwriter son Hoyt Axton.

pared a thing for him to eat! So she and I got busy making his favorite meal of beans, potatoes and, of course, cornbread. I don't think we even had a meat dish of any kind.

We had it ready soon after he got home and we all sat down to eat. Mae left the table to go into another room to watch the show that Hoyt had filmed earlier that day. Hoyt and I stayed in the dining room and talked, while having dinner. We had such a great conversation. I felt this was the first time that I had really gotten to know him. He was a big ol' teddy bear type and very nice.

Mae was so proud of her son and rightly so! At one time, Hoyt could be heard on most of the McDonald commercials and he appeared on *Nashville Now*, hosted by Ralph Emery, on many occasions. Hoyt, like his brother John, loved their Mom and if I didn't like him for any other reason, I would have liked him for that. But I did and I admired his many talents. He was an actor and in the movies "The Gremlins" and my favorite, "The Black Stallion."

Hoyt was also a talented songwriter with many hits under his belt, such as "Rusty Old Halo" (he did not write that song) and the smash hit (he wrote) by Three Dog Night, "Joy To The World," which some call *Jeremiah Was a Bullfrog.* He was a son, a dad and a friend. I'm honored to have been counted among his many friends. Hoyt went home to be with the Lord, Oct. 26, 1999, at age 61.

VIC McALPIN ...

I mention Vic McAlpin in the Johnny Russell story, but I feel that his story needs to also be told and remembered. Vic is yet another "legend." It's true that he wasn't a performing artist or a star. Neither was he a songwriter-turned-performer, but he was a terrific songwriter and one heck of a nice guy, and I felt fortunate to have had him as my friend.

Mary Reeves and Vic McAlpin.

Vic wrote for Acclaim Music, Inc., a Jim Reeves Enterprises company, for about the last 15 years of his life, and while he was with Acclaim, he wrote such songs as "Jackson Ain't A Very Big Town," a hit by Johnny and June Carter Cash; "What Locks The Door," charted by Jack Greene; and Nat Stuckey had a hit recording of Vic's "Plastic Saddle."

Before Vic began writing for Acclaim, he had already enjoyed many years of success with such hits as "Almost," which he co-written with Jack Toombs and was first popularized by George Morgan in 1952. Some will remember Vic's oldie, but goodie, "Give Me An RC Cola And A Moon Pie." This one is rather special to me.

One year for my birthday when we had the office at RCA, some friends of mine took me to lunch. There was Vicky Mabe Vaughn, Dot Boys who worked for RCA, Vic, Eddie Miller (writer of "Release Me"), myself and Robbie Robinson. We went to what was then a very nice place called The Executive Club. We ate and pretty soon Eddie Miller just up and left the table. When he came back, he had a Moon Pie. He said that he couldn't find any cake to help me celebrate, so that would have to do. It was such a fun time. A Moon Pie is only about four inches in diameter. Somewhere he found a little birthday candle and they lit it and all sang "Happy Birthday" to me and then we cut the Moon Pie into six little pieces, allowing me to share one of the most fun birthdays that I have ever had. That's one that has been more meaningful than most any other one that I've had except for my 50th. It was just the right thing to have since Vic had written that song.

For about five years while at RCA, Vic also worked out of our office. We became very close, as people do working with one another the way we did. Vic shared many wonderful stories with me during this time. Stories about Hank Williams, Fred Rose, George Morgan, and many of the other "greats" that were in the music business so many years ago. Hank Williams and Vic were fishing buddies and I am so happy that he shared many of his memories about Hank with me, as Hank was also one of my favorites. In March, after he died on Jan. 1, 1953, one of the local radio stations in Louisville had a *Hank Williams' Day,* where they only played his recordings all day. Along with some of my girl friends, we skipped school that day to just listen to his music!

Everyone on Music Row knew Vic. I don't think there was an office that he couldn't walk into and see who he wanted to see. They not only knew him, they loved him, as well. Vic always looked like he stepped out of a page of a men's clothing catalog. He was one of the sharpest dressers that I have ever known in my life, and one of the nicest people that I have had the pleasure of knowing. We shared many good times working together and I treasure my memories of him. I loved him and miss him very much. (Vic passed away in January 1980.)

MAC WISEMAN ...

Mac Wiseman, a Bluegrass Hall of Honor member, is one of those people that I've known since 1958; yet, I don't know a great deal about him. I do know that he is a super nice man, and always good for a laugh. I suppose he is most noted for his recording of "Jimmy Brown, The Newsboy," but he has enjoyed many great recordings when he was an artist on Dot Records, including "Tis Sweet To Be Remembered" and "Love

Mac Wiseman and Joyce are not camera-shy.

Letters In the Sand."

It was right after I started working for Jim that Mac came into our office in Primrose Center, and we have been friends all these many years, but since we didn't have the same circle of friends, I never got to k now him very well, except that I love him. Charlie Dick, Mac and I all went to the funeral services for Chet Atkins, which was held at the Ryman Auditorium, and I remember asking Mac if he remembered when we first met and he told me the exact time.

Well, that made me feel very special, for many years had passed at that time since our first meeting. Mac is one of the people that I have had the privilege of knowing, yet not knowing very well at all. You're a jewel Mac, and a very special man.

ARCHIE CAMPBELL ...

Archie Campbell was one of the funniest men I ever met, and one of the nicest. Archie's office was just down the hall from us in the RCA Building, and we always had such a good time. His son Steve worked for him, and Steve was another extremely nice guy. I don't want to leave out Phillip, Archie's other son. He was also very nice, but I knew Steve better than I did Phillip.

Their dad, of course, was a regular performer and writer for the TV classic series *Hee Haw* and when my daughter Joy was about 5 years old, Archie invited us to the set and that was really a blast. Archie picked Joy up and carried her around most of the time that we were there. That's when I met The Hager Twins. (I met them again some years later in Billings, during Montana's 1989 Centennial.)

Archie became a part of the Opry cast in 1958, and that pretty much filled the gap that was left by Rod Brasfield. I personally don't think anyone could fill Rod's place, but Archie surely did a good job (and he performed a satirical piece titled "Rindercella," a hilarious take-off on the fairy tale classic "Cinderella"). For RCA , he recorded some serious duets with Lorene Mann, including their Top 20 single "The Dark End Of the Street" in 1968. (In his later years, he also co-hosted TNN's *Yesteryear in Nashville* series.)

The Opry and *Hee Haw* lost him on Aug. 29, 1987, when he died at age 72, leaving a void that cannot be replaced in our industry. I still miss him and often reflect back to our fun times in the halls on the third floor of that old RCA Building.

GEORGE HAMILTON IV ...

Can't remember just when I first met George Hamilton IV, but it was before he moved to Nashville in the Autumn of 1959. He's another really nice guy. George came out to visit the Jim Reeves Museum one time; however, I was not there, but he wrote me the nicest letter praising the museum. I have often wondered why he wrote me instead of Mary, but perhaps he also wrote her. I never heard her say, though I did show her the letter he wrote, and she did not say that she had received one.

George and I basically knew each other just as business friends and we always had good conversations backstage at the *Grand Ole Opry,* but we really didn't do things together, as I have with so many of my country music friends. George has enjoyed many hit recordings and I admire him so much as an artist and as a person. His hits include "A Rose And A Baby Ruth," "Abilene" and "Break My Mind."

Like Jim, he is very popular in England and other countries of Europe. George, I appreciate you as a gentleman, an artist and as my friend.

George Hamilton IV with the author's daughter Joy.

DARRELL McCALL ...

To me, Darrell McCall has one of the greatest voices ever, but he just never made it big as a single artist. I always thought he was so handsome, too, and even though we never dated, we did do a little smooching from time-to-time. Yes, he was a good kisser!

I got to know Darrell shortly after he and Johnny Paycheck (then Donny Young) came to town. It wasn't long after that time period that he began touring with both Faron Young, as his drummer, and Ray Price as a harmony singer. He later became the tenor singer with the group,"

Darrell also recorded some duets with Willie Nelson and Curtis Potter. Curtis is another one of those fine singers that although he has enjoyed some success (such as the 1963 Top 20 single "A Stranger Was Here"), just never made it as a big artist. He was on RCA Records for a short time and that's when I met him, as Ray Pennington was his producer, and one of the RCA producers then.

I saw Darrell at a press conference that Ralph held for one of his books. I believe it was for his (1992) book titled "Memories: The Autobiography of Ralph Emery." Both Darrell and I were acknowledged as helping to give Ralph some information that he included in his memoirs. He mentioned me first and I got to tell Darrell that I had top billing over him, and we had a good laugh about it. His wife Mona was with him and I told her that I had always loved Darrell, and she was so cute with her answer to me and said she could understand that because she loved him, too.

During one of the parties that we both attended, which I believe was at Charlie Moseley's house, Darrell and I went out to his car and that's when I first learned what a good kisser he was! It was a very warm night and Darrell had on this peach-colored Western shirt along with a T-shirt, and he took the Western shirt off and I told him I wanted it, so I could always remember him. He gave it to me then and there, and Darrell, I still have that shirt. It even has your last name on the inside collar. I think it must have been from one of the cleaners that you had taken it to. Boy, were you small then! But a lot of us were smaller then! That had to have been somewhere around 1959 or early 1960.

I love both you and Mona, Darrell, and because I got to know you, I now treasure another beautiful memory.

BOB LUMAN ...

Bob Luman was a good friend of Dean Manuel's (Jim's pianist) and that's how I first met him. Dean brought him by the office probably in 1962. Seems they had been in service together, as best I can recall.

I know I was happy to meet him, because after hearing Bob sing his big hit "Let's Think About Living," I became a fan. What a great song! He later had a big hit with "Lonely Women Make Good Lovers."

After I met Bob, it seemed that every time I went to the airport to either take someone or pick someone up, I would run into him. It got to be a joke between us that we had to stop meeting like that! He was always friendly and although I never did get to know him personally, I am thankful for the time I did know Bob Luman.

I also met his wife Barbara at Mae Axton's home when she hosted the media get-together for the viewing of the Bill Rains' sculpture, "Journey To Graceland," depicting the three phases of Elvis Presley's life. She's a very sweet lady and I was also happy to meet her and tell her how much I had admired Bob's talent.

Sadly, Bob contracted pneumonia and died on Dec. 27, 1978. He was only 41 years old.

BOBBY LORD ...

One of the things that I remember best about Bobby Lord is that he was a wonderful story-teller and boy did he have 'em!

When we shared guest spots on Ralph Emery's late night radio program one time, Bobby told one of the funniest stories that I have ever heard. Bobby said that whenever he was on tour he would always try to find out where a church was that was predominately black, because he said he knew he would always find a funny story there. The story he told me was no different. The best I remember, he said he was someplace in Michigan and found this black church. It was cold and had snowed and there was snow and ice on the church steps, so he said he just parked the car not far from the church to just watch for a while. Pretty soon this heavy-set lady started up the steps of the church and he said when she reached about the fifth step, she slipped and literally bounced all the way down to the bottom! When she got up, he said she turned around and pointed her finger to the steps, and said, "July's gonna get you!" That's the meanest thing the churchgoer could think of to say to the steps! Maybe you had to be there and hear Bobby tell it, but it was so funny! Hope you will agree.

Bobby had a pretty big hit called "Without Your Love," a Top 10 written by Wanda Jackson, and he worked with Red Foley on the ABC *Jubilee USA* network TV show in the late 1950's and then had his own long-running syndicated TV series in the late 1960's.

Miss your stories Bobby, and I thank God that he allowed our paths to cross. Bobby Lord died Feb. 16, 2008, following a lengthy illness. He was 74.

JOHNNY CASH ...

Johnny and Joyce.

When I attended the *Midnight Jamboree* at E.T.'s Record Shop in 1957, Johnny Cash was the show's main guest artist. I had the opportunity backstage to visit a little bit with Johnny Cash and had a picture made with him.

After moving to Nashville and after he married June Carter, I used to run into him quite a bit at the bank and he was always friendly. He knew my face and that I worked for Jim. Then I met him another time when he stopped by Margie and Luther Perkins' home while I was visiting them. We all talked for a little while and I got to know him a little better.

On Jim's album, "The Best Of Jim Reeves, Vol. III," Johnny wrote the liner notes for us. I used to go to his TV shows and was always amazed at the electricity that seemed to emanate from him

to his audience. He had such charisma! Bill Walker, who wrote the movie score for Jim's movie "Kimberley Jim," was Johnny's orchestra leader. What a wonderful pair of talented men! I'm so glad that I knew Johnny, but wish I could have known both he and June better. They are both gone now, she having died May 15, 2003, and only months later, Johnny passed away on Sept. 12.

DON HELMS ...

Steel guitarist Don Helms was one of Hank Williams' original Drifting Cowboys, and a regular guy, to boot. I was saddened to learn of his death on Aug. 11, 2008, as the industry lost one of the best steel players ever (except for my brother-in-law Stu). In fact, Stu and Don were very good friends and some people thought they looked enough alike that they got them mixed up a lot.

There was a men's clothing store at Rivergate Mall in Madison, and both Don and Stu shopped there, using the same clerk to wait on them and he always got them confused. They pulled a trick on him one time and both of them went in together. The man didn't know what to say to either of them. Wish I'd been there to have seen the look that I'm sure he had on his face.

When Jeanie and Frank Oakley and I put together the first Willie Nelson Museum, I went to Don and asked him if he would like to be a part of the museum, and if so, would he loan us something notable to place in the museum depicting the fact that he had been with Hank's original band. He let us use the steel guitar that he had used in Hank's band and I remember him telling us to be very careful with it, because next to Hazel, his wonderful, sweet wife, this guitar was his most valued possession. He later got the guitar back when we moved the museum to the Music Valley area near Opryland.

Gordon Terry, Ron Elliott and Don Helms.

Don more or less retired from playing and the only times that I would run into him and Hazel would be when one of our industry people had passed away, and it was always such a pleasure to see them both even during some of those saddest times. It got to be a standard joke that we had to quit meeting at funeral homes.

One time Teddy and Doyle were to play the Kentucky State Fair and they asked if I would like to ride to Louisville with them, as they knew I'd be able to see my Mom and of course, I jumped at the chance. Don was working with them at their Sure-Fire Music Publishing Company, and he went along. Don and I sat in the back seat and all the way to Louisville, he quoted limericks. He was the very best when it came to citing limericks. That was such a fun trip. I laughed most of the entire time. This was the same trip where Teddy, my sister Marsha (who still lived with Mom), George Jones and me all went out to the Midway and rode that Wild Mouse. I loved Don and Hazel and will miss him just knowing he's not with us, but the industry has surely lost one of its greats.

JOHNNY RODRIGUEZ ...

Hey, I was fortunate to be able to work on Johnny Rodriguez's 1972 breakthrough Top 10 "Pass Me By," as we were administering Tom T. Hall's publishing company at that time, and this was one of their songs.

Later, we visited at a party in Jack Johnson's home. Jack was Johnny's manager and it was a fun gathering. I told Johnny about working on his record and during the course of our conversation, we got away from the main crowd and went into another area of the house. That's when I got my first and only kiss from Johnny. He, too, was a great kisser!

I did not see him again for a number of years, but followed his career, as I felt he was a wonderful talent. Then, during one of the Fan Fairs, I ran into him again. In fact, it was at the International Fan Club Organization's show when Lana Nelson accepted the Ernest Tubb Humanitarian Award for her dad, Willie Nelson. Bill Rains, who sculpted this award, was there with his wife Melissa. I had just been telling Melissa how Johnny and I sneaked off, and I got my kiss, because she mentioned to me how much she liked him. He kept looking over at me and Melissa, and finally he came over and said, "I think I know you." I told him he did and refreshed his memory of the time at Jack's house and, of course, then he also remembered!

That's about the extent of my knowing Johnny, but what a pleasant memory, and

I am extremely glad we became acquainted, though only briefly. Sometimes brief is good! Thanks Johnny.

DEL REEVES ...

Dean Manuel brought Del Reeves to our office at Jim Reeves Enterprises, long before his move to Nashville in 1962, when he was urged to do so by his friend Hank Cochran. At the time, Del may have just been in town to record for Decca (where he recorded the hits "Be Quiet Mind" and "He Stands Real Tall").

At any rate, Del switched labels and began having United Artists' hit recordings, most notably the #1 "Girl On The Billboard." About four years after he and wife Ellen first came to Nashville, Del joined the *Grand Ole Opry.*

Del was always a fun person to be around and one night I was at the *Friday Night Opry* and Del and I were talking, and I told him that I had cooked some cabbage earlier that day. How we got on the subject of cooking, I don't know; but Del said he loved cooked cabbage and had not had any in a long time. I told him mine was seasoned fairly hot, and he said it didn't get too hot for him, so I told him to come by the house after he finished his portion of the show. He said he would and did, and after a few bites of cabbage and cornbread, he admitted that it was a little too hot, even for him. We had a good laugh about it and every time I would see him after that, he would ask if I had cooked any more cabbage.

It sure made a good memory for me, and although our paths crossed many times during the time that I lived in Nashville, I believe having that cabbage together was the only time that we actually shared any one-on-one time together. I loved Del's unique style of singing and his wonderful sense of humor, and was saddened when he departed, as were many others. I'm glad I could have this memory of him to share. Del died Jan. 1, 2007, at age 74.

MAC DAVIS ...

It was at one of the Celebrity Golf Tournaments during the 1970s' DJ Convention when I first met Mac Davis. I can't pin-point the exact year, but that's not important. But being able to talk with Mac, though briefly, was important to me. The last time that I was able to visit with him again was in 2006 in Carthage, when he was inducted into the Texas Country Music Hall of Fame. Mogens and Hanne Jensen, friends of mine from Copenhagen, Denmark, and Jim's niece, Lana Arnold and me, all attended the festivities the night of his induction and Mac performed. Johnny Lee also sang that night, along with his beautiful daughter. I know many will remember his #1 duet with Lane Brody, titled "The Yellow Rose (of Texas)."

Mac was so much fun to watch and, of course, he's written so many wonderful hit recordings such as "In The Ghetto" and "Don't Cry, Daddy" for Elvis Presley. However, I like the way Mac does them, along with his own recordings of "Texas In My Rear View Mirror" and "It's Hard To Be Humble."

Mac Davis is such a talent and an equally nice guy. Now he says that he has retired, but not to worry about him, as he is doing OK, and I believe that! I am so thankful that I can add Mac to the ones that I have come to know in this wonderful, wacky world of music.

ROY DRUSKY ...

Roy was one of the sweetest men in the music industry. He was very quiet and a little shy, but I used to go to the Opry and go in the back door and there would be Roy and his wife Bobbie, sitting there talking with the back-door guard, Mr. Norman Van Dame. Most of the time, there would not be anyone else around and I would always go over and visit with them for a while. They were both so nice and when Roy passed on Sept. 23, 2004, Charlie Dick and I went to his memorial service and while waiting to go into the church, Bobbie came over to me and told me she was so glad that I could make it. I was surprised that she remembered me, as it has been some time since I had seen either of them, especially since Roy had become so ill.

I'm told that Roy had emphysema and that this is what he ultimately died from, but I'm not sure about that. I am sure that Roy was a tremendous artist and sang ballads, much like Jim Reeves and Eddy Arnold, with such hits as "Second Hand Rose," "Another" and one of my favorites, his novelty song "Peel Me A Nanner" (written by Bill Anderson) and the one that always tugged at my heart, "Jody And The Kid," which was written by Kris Kristofferson. (Roy was also a songwriter in his own right, as he wrote Faron Young's two #1 hits, "Alone With You" and "Country Girl.")

Roy, I sure do miss our many conversations at the back-door lounge.

CARL PERKINS ...

Carl Perkins was someone I only met once, but I loved his rockabilly-style music. Lee Rosenberg and I were down at Linebaugh's one night when Carl came in with Luther Perkins (no relation). Luther was Johnny Cash's guitar picker. They were very good friends and later on Carl toured a great deal with Johnny. All were part of the early Memphis scene.

They joined us, as they knew Lee, but this was the first time that I met either of them. Luther and I became good friends after he married Margie Higgins. Carl had a record that had just been released, and they wanted us to take a ride out Gallatin Road to see someone, and it might have been Carl's promoter. I just don't remember exactly who, but we said we'd go with them and had to walk a few blocks to where Carl's car was parked. It was in a parking lot and when we got to it and sat in, Carl asked if I'd like one of his pictures that had just been made. I said I did, and Carl signed it to me, though the signature isn't visible here.

When we got out on Gallatin Road, we saw that there was a fire and we kidded Carl and said he must really have a hot record to have it cause a fire. We all had a good laugh and a really fun time, and I'm sorry that I did not get to know Carl Perkins better. (He was inducted into the Rock & Roll Hall of Fame in 1987; and died of a stroke, Jan. 19, 1998, at age 65.)

LORETTA LYNN ...

Loretta Lynn and I met about the first night she was in Nashville. Don't know how she met Teddy and Doyle, but they brought her to *The Midnight Jamboree,* so Loretta could sing, and gave up one of their spots for her to do so. I believe she told me that this was the first time she had sung on a radio station as powerful as WSM. I got to know her pretty good over the years and, of course, she became a tremendous success. She traveled with The Wilburn Brothers and was a regular on their TV show for quite some time. She became friends with Patsy Cline, who also helped in guiding her early career. When she had her identical twins, Patsy and Peggy, Charlie Dick and I went to see her in the hospital. Patsy had been gone over a year at that time. (This was Aug. 6, 1964.)

We ran into each other on many occasions, but one night when she was to appear on the Opry, Joy and I went, but Joy did not know that I knew Loretta. Joy grew up around all these people and she knew that I worked with and knew many of them, but we didn't really discuss this fact at home. Anyway, we went to Loretta's dressing room, as I hadn't seen her in quite some time, and she jumped up and came over and gave me a hug. We had a good time talking and reminiscing a bit, and Joy said, "Mom, I didn't know you knew her!" Loretta got a big laugh out of that, and told Joy that we went back many years.

I have a lot of memories of Loretta when she would appear on *The Midnight Jamboree.* She did that a lot early in her career and we had many talks backstage. She did some duets with Ernest Tubb, but most of the major duets she did were with Conway Twitty, and they were always hits. Songs like "Louisiana Woman, Mississippi Man," which was written by my friend, Jim Owen. Jim's wife Yvette and I were very close friends. One of my favorite Conway-Loretta duets was "After The Fire Is Gone."

Margaret Kozelle, a fan, with Jim and Loretta.

I have not seen Loretta for quite some time, but have kept up with her career over the years through her recordings, but also through the Johnson Sisters, Loudilla, Kay and Loretta, who jointly were a vital part of Loretta's career as her fan club presidents and as presidents of IFCO. These girls have done so much to promote not only Loretta, but have been responsible for helping to launch others on their way up the success ladder. I'm also happy my path of life crossed these girls' paths.

Loretta wrote many of her hits, and two of my very favorites are "You Ain't Woman Enough" and "Coal Miner's Daughter." This one was also the title of the book and movie about Loretta's life (which starred Sissy Spacek). It was a very good movie, but veered away from the truth a bit, especially after Loretta's move to Nashville.

I miss our talks Loretta, but I am thankful that I have so many memories of you and can share a few of them. Love you, my fellow Kentuckian!

SKEETER DAVIS …

I must have met Skeeter Davis soon after I began working for Jim, as it seems like I knew her from the time I went to Nashville, until she passed away on Sept. 19, 2004. I got the news of her death while I was visiting some fans of Jim's, Mogens and Hanne Jensen in Copenhagen, Denmark. They had flown me and Jim's niece, Lani Arnold, over there. They have become such wonderful friends of mine, more like family than friends. I was able to be home in time to attend Skeeter's funeral, which was held at the Ryman Auditorium. Charlie Dick and I went together. Seems like Charlie and I did that a lot! I loved Skeeter and know she loved me, too. Her sister Doozie ran around with us girls and many times Skeeter joined in our fun times.

We have shared many wonderful talks together about many things, but one of our best subjects was our Lord and Savior, Jesus Christ. She loved the Lord and was ridiculed on several occasions for her strong faith and beliefs. Some will remember when she was suspended for about 15 months, before finally getting back on the show, just because she stood up for Jesus, and the people that were at that time doing His work.

Skeeter will always be remembered for her wonderful duet "I've Forgot More Than You'll Ever Know" with Betty Jack Davis, known together as The Davis Sisters; and who could ever forget her version of "The Last Date," which was such a monster hit by Floyd Cramer. Most will remember Skeeter's classic hit "The End Of The World." What a great record!

She gave me a copy of her book "Bus Fare to Kentucky," Dec. 18, 1993, and wrote a nice message for me. There were some things I did not know about her, and I felt I got to know her even better after reading her book. I miss you Skeeter and like you, I love our Lord and Savior, Jesus Christ.

Merry Christmas 1995

Bus Fare to Kentucky

Joyce and Skeeter backstage.

*Joyce —
I hope you like my life story — maybe you'll find something in here you didn't know — even though we've been friends for years. Love & joy Skeeter Davis
12-18-93*

JEANNIE SEELY ...

Jeannie Seely first came to Nashville in 1965, and we met right afterwards. She said it was at the DJ Convention of that year. She was good friends with Gail Talley (writer of "Not Until The Next Time" which Jim Reeves recorded) and Gail was the one who introduced us, and we've been friends all these years. If you have never seen her perform, then you should, as she is a real entertainer, not just a terrific singer, which she is, with hits like "Don't Touch Me," but she really knows how to connect with her audience.

Even though I've known Jeannie a long time, we really never did things together, but whenever or wherever I'd see her, she was always the same. I loved this about her and she was always friendly with me.

Jeannie traveled the road with Jack Greene for a time, and they recorded together, but a couple of my favorite Jeannie Seely recordings are "Wish I Didn't Have To Miss You" and "Can I Sleep in Your Arms (Tonight)" and I loved her comedic recording of :"We're Still Hangin' In There, Ain't We Jessi." This is the song where she says at this writing, she's Hank's #4 and she is referring to Jessi Colter, who was married to

Jeannie and Joyce at SOURCE Awards gala, July 2009.

Waylon Jennings (and earlier to Duane Eddy).

Jeannie is also a songwriter and has had several recorded by other artists, and one such song that comes to mind is "It Just Takes Practice" recorded by Dottie West. (She also acted on stage in the late-1980's, playing various acting roles: She was Miss Mona in "The Best Little Whorehouse in Texas" and played Jean Shepard's daughter and Lorrie Morgan's mother in the musical "Takin' It Home.") Love you Jeannie, and keep hangin' in there.

SHEB WOOLEY ...

Sheb Wooley I did not know well, but came into contact with on several occasions. One of those times was when he helped out on the Hands Across The Table charity in Billings. Sheb was on the show, along with other Nashville entertainers, such as Jack Greene, Norma Jean, Jan Howard and Johnny Russell. I was handling the celebrity auction, so got to know Sheb and his wife Linda a little better than I would have otherwise.

Joyce and Sheb.

Sheb was such a versatile talent. Who could forget his pop hit "Purple People Eater" (or country hits like "That's My Pa!"). As his alter ego, Ben Colder, he enjoyed novelty successes, such as the Top 10 "Almost Persuaded #2."Actor Sheb played Pete Nolan in the Clint Eastwood TV series *Rawhide,* and was the bad guy menacing Gary Cooper in the classic Western, "High Noon." He was also the writer of the theme song for the TV show *Hee Haw* that lasted a quarter of a century. Loved that show. (Sheb died Sept. 16, 2003, at age 82.)

NORMA JEAN ...

Norma Jean was known by everyone in the music business as *Pretty Miss Norma Jean* and she deserved that name, as she is a very beautiful lady. I met her while she was a regular on *The Porter Wagoner Show,* which lasted about seven years, but didn't get to know her better until she later left that show and went back to Norman, Okla.

In 1971, Joy and I went to Phoenix and on to San Diego to visit with my aunt and uncle, and we stopped by Norma Jean's home in Norman on our way out and visited for a while. I remember her daughter Roma and Joy playing together, while Norma and I visited. I thought she had the most beautiful bathroom that I had ever seen.

After she moved back to Nashville, I saw her quite a bit at the ROPE meetings. During this time she married writer-musician George Riddle, who used to travel a lot with George Jones and sang harmony with him. He and Bill Carlisle were also very close friends and he sang with him on the Opry, during most of Bill's latter years.

Norma Jean was also among some of the other Nashville talents that helped out with the Hands Across The Table charity in Montana. Norma now lives in Branson, Mo., and has remarried. She and her husband pastor a nondenominational church there called The Cowboy Church. Norma is a very special lady and I am so happy that our paths crossed those many years ago, You are still *Pretty Miss Norma Jean.*

Norma Jean welcomes Joyce Jackson.

Jumpin' Bill Carlisle with Norma Jean and then-husband George Riddle.

JERRY REED ...

Jerry and Joyce

What a talent Jerry Reed was: guitar player, singer, songwriter, actor, husband, father . . . and I suppose I could add more to the list, if I thought about it. Jerry and I weren't really close friends at all; however, we used to talk a lot in and around the studio at RCA. What a character! I loved his zest for life, and he was always in a laughing mood. Wish I had gotten to know him better, but I treasure the little chats that we did have, and know that he is loved by so many friends and fans around the world. I loved him as the Snowman in "Smoky and The Bandit," which co-starred Burt Reynolds and Jerry. I suppose his biggest hit was one of my favorites, titled "When You're Hot, You're Hot." However, I also liked "She Got The Gold Mine, I Got The Shaft."

Like I said, what a talent! Sadly, Jerry died Sept. 1, 2008, and he was 71.

T. G. SHEPPARD ...

I got to know T.G. Sheppard even before he became that popular recording artist. I first knew him as Bill Browder, RCA's promotion man from Memphis, when he used to come to the label in Nashville. He was good friends with Elroy Kahanek who had taken Wally Cochran's place as Nashville promotion man. Yvette Owen was Elroy's secretary, and we were really good friends. (Yvette passed away in 2005, from a long battle with breast cancer. I still miss her very much.)

Under the stage name, T.G. Sheppard, his first charting was a #1 hit titled, "Devil In The Bottle." He was always so very nice to me and I loved talking with him and was happy for his success. The last time I talked with T.G. was when Dottie West died in that terrible car accident. I was working for Mae Axton at DPI Records and T.G. knew that Dottie and I had been friends and called to ask me about her funeral arrangements.

We didn't have the same circle of friends, although I would often see and chat with him at one function or another, but knowing him through RCA was about as far as our friendship went. But I am very glad I knew him, because T.G. you really are a super guy and another that should wear the proverbial white hat . . . Thanks for the memories.

CONWAY TWITTY ...

Conway Twitty is another of those persons who crossed my path but briefly. I had seen him perform many times and also attended the Grammy Awards when it was held in Nashville, where he and Loretta Lynn performed. But when I really got to meet and talk with him was when he opened up Twitty City near Hendersonville, Tenn.

I had met Mickey, his wife at that time, and Mike, his son, as they had come by our Jim Reeves Museum wanting to get a few pointers about starting their museum and other businesses within their Twitty City complex. I gave them a tour and when Conway opened Twitty City, I was invited to the opening. Conway and I visited for quite some time and he thanked me for showing his family around our museum. We just chatted in general, but what a hitmaker Conway was with 40 #1 songs like "Hello Darlin'," "Linda On My Mind" and, of course, the pop smash that made him a Rock & Roll pioneer, "It's Only Make Believe." The industry truly lost a definiive artist when we lost Conway.Twitty. An aneurysm prompted his death on June 5, 1993, at age 59. (He was inducted posthumously into the Country Music Hall of Fame in 1999.)

KATHERINE SUTCLIFFE ...

First I would like to start out saying, "I love you Kathy, so much, and our friendship has always been so special to me." It all started in 1990, when Ruby Taylor gave me a book that Katherine had written titled "A Fire In The Heart." I wrote her and she wrote me back, and later when she planned a trip to Nashville, she let me know and Ruby and I went to meet her. We became instant friends and whenever she would come to Nashville, she would stay with either Ruby or me. I loved those times spent with her.

Once when she was visiting in Nashville, she, Ruby and I went on a dinner train to celebrate one of my birthdays. It was The Broadway Dinner Train and we had a wonderful evening.

Another time when she was in town, Ruby, Mae Axton, Katherine and I all went for an evening on the General Jackson (a showboat that sails the Cumberland River). That night someone gave each of us a rose, and I made the statement, "Guess any time is a time for roses." Katherine was in the process of writing a new book, which she said was the sequel to "A Fire In The Heart" and asked me if I would write a poem for the front of the book. She had read some of my poems and liked them. I loved writing poems, but had never been asked to do it professionally for anyone, but I told her that I would be honored to do so. The poem I wrote is titled "A Time For Roses" and it lends itself to the storyline of her book. I did have it all wrong at first, but she sent me an incomplete manuscript of the book, so I could get the feel of the story and I wrote the poem and it is in her book titled "My Only Love." So, because of Katherine, I am a published poet! Here is the poem:

A TIME FOR ROSES
By Joyce Jackson
January 1993

A ROSE JUST MIGHT BE TAKEN FOR DEAD
WHEN COVERED WITH LEAVES OR WINTER'S SNOW
BUT WHEN IT'S AGAIN A TIME FOR ROSES
THAT ROSE WILL SPRING FORTH AND GROW

HURT CAN BE HIDDEN, SO NO ONE CAN SEE
WHEN COVERED WITH FEAR OR WITH HATE
BUT LOVE CAN ERASE ALL THAT IS HIDDEN
IF YOU JUST LET IT, BEFORE IT'S TOO LATE

DON'T LET THE ANGER OF YOUR TORTURED SOUL
BLIND YOU TO WHAT SURELY CAN BE
LOVE THAT'S AS FRESH AS A RAIN-DRENCHED ROSE
JUST MIGHT HAPPEN BETWEEN YOU AND ME

I MAY NOT BE THE ONE YOU HAD CHOSEN
AND YOU'RE NOT THE ONE I WOULD CLAIM
BUT SOMETIMES LIFE DEALS US A HAND
AND WE PLAY IT TO STAY IN THE GAME

SO WHAT MAY NOW SEEM HIDDEN OR DEAD
LIKE THE ROSES WAITING FOR SPRING
OUR LOVE COULD BLOOM, IF GIVEN A CHANCE
WHEN IT'S TIME FOR ROSES AGAIN

Katherine and Guy Davis (a model for some of Katherine's books) were on a book promotion tour and when they came to Nashville; they both stayed with me. That was one of the most fun times that I have ever had. Guy was a barrel of fun and I gave up my bedroom for him and Katherine, and I had to sleep on my pull-out hide-a-bed. We told each other some of our life stories and laughed our heads off, but what a precious memory that was and still is, when I remember it from time-to-time.

Katherine has been a *New York Times'* best selling author and has written many, many best sellers. The last time that we corresponded, she told me she had changed from writing historical romance novels to writing suspense-mystery novels. To date, I haven't read any of those, but I know they will be good ones, as "good" is the only way Katherine writes!

Hope readers enjoy some of the photos of Katherine and myself, as well as those others with Ruby, Kitty and Mama Mae. What a special person you are to me Kathy. As I said on the dedication page, you'll just never know what having you as a friend has meant to me. You are a real treasure and I love you and value your friendship so much.

Best-selling novelist Katherine Sutcliffe.

Joyce and Katherine.

*Good friends
Joyce and Kath-
erine.*

BILL RAINS ...

Artist, sculptor, used-to-be barber, as well as father, husband and a friend to many. That's Bill Rains. But, this is my book, and I claim his friendship here. The year was 1975, and Mae Axton brought him to Nashville and introduced him to Mary Reeves and her Jim Reeves Enterprises' staff. Mine and Bill's friendship has grown since then to what is now more or less a family thing. In fact, Bill says I am part of his family and a big part of his history. I treasure him feeling that way, but really I have never done much, except be there for him.

One of Bill's dreams was to sculpt country artists in bronze, so they would always be remembered and Mary was the first one to commission him to do a bronze of Jim Reeves. Back then it was only 30 inches high, but the likeness was incredible! Hardly anyone has been able to capture Jim's likeness in a drawing or painting, but Bill did in bronze. Betty Harper is the only other artist that I feel captured Jim as he should be, but hers were sketches and totally different.

Later, Bill started doing larger-than-life size bronzes and to date has done Ernest Tubb, Keith Whitley, Hank Williams, Sr., Buck Owens, Johnny Cash, Hank Snow, Merle Haggard, Minnie Pearl, George Jones and Garth Brooks. He also did a three-phase bronze of Elvis, depicting the three stages of his career titled "Journey To Graceland." I mentioned this in Mae Axton's story because Mae kept it at her home, until it was time to take it to Graceland. This was in January 1986, and unveiled on Elvis' birthday on Jan. 8th. I was part of all that back then, as Bill, his wife Melissa and their son Dustin, spent the night with me, and we put a U-Haul behind my old Pontiac station-wagon and took it to Memphis. What a fun time for all of us.

When they spent the night, we had finished with our dinner and somehow Bill broke the ear-piece off his glasses. There was no place to get them repaired, so I gave him some super glue with the hope that it would work until he could get somewhere and get them repaired. We left him at the kitchen table and Melissa and I went into anoth-

*Bill with David McCormick
at the Johnny Cash statue.*

er room to talk and get better acquainted, when we heard Bill yell for us to come to the kitchen. When we got in there, Bill had his ear-piece glued to the other part of the glasses, but he had also glued his finger to the ear-piece and couldn't get it off! We all laughed our heads off, and we still laugh about that to this day.

Bill and Melissa hosted an unveiling in Montana for his friends and family there of "Journey To Graceland," and I along with Mae was fortunate enough to be present there. Graceland's director, Jack Soden, and Todd Morgan, Graceland's communications director, came to Billings from Memphis for that unveiling as well.

I love Montana and all the wonderful people that I have met through my association with Bill and Melissa. Friends such as Denny and P.J. Eubank, Charlean Keller (Charlean has since passed away), all of Bill's children and their families and so many other fun people. David McCormick, owner of The Ernest Tubb Record Shops, commissioned Bill to sculpt the Ernest Tubb Humanitarian award that was to be given away during the Fan Fair event to someone who had helped further another's career and who had been helpful to mankind. Willie Nelson got this first award, designed as a small head likeness of Ernest Tubb.

Willie was not able to come to Fan Fair that year, but his daughter Lana came on his behalf and accepted the award. There was an unveiling of Keith Whitley in Nashville, which I attended. They took that bronze to Kentucky, where Keith is buried. Keith, as many of you will remember, was married to Lorrie Morgan; both are tremendous talents. The night that Hank Williams, Sr., was unveiled was when Jett Williams and Hank, Jr. met for the first time. (They are half brother and sister). It was quite an evening! A few years later, three more of his bigger-than-life bronzes were unveiled at the Ryman Auditorium. Unveiled were Johnny Cash, Hank Snow and Buck Owens. Many were on hand for that unveiling, as well. Again, I was honored to be invited to attend.

Bill does such a tremendous job of intricately detailing even minor features on these bronzes. One always seem better than the next. I am in awe of his talent, as well as the talent of his entire family. What a legacy he will be leaving!

He not only has done the bronzes of some of the country music artists, but he has done some of the real old Western characters, as well, such as Wild Bill Hickok and the wild life that has and still does roam the west.

Recently, Bill completed a major life-size bronze of Dave McNally, left-handed pitcher of the Baltimore Orioles, who is from Billings, and I was invited to be present for the unveiling on June 29, 2008. It was such a wonderful event and I met and was invited to Dave's widow Jean McNally's home later that day. It was all so much fun, and wonderful to be with Bill and Melissa again as a guest in their home. I have written the following poem about Montana , showing how I feel about this state and its people. I was so honored to be invited to be a part of Montana's Centennial cattle drive that started in Roundup, and ended with driving herds of both longhorn and shorthorn cattle, down Billings' main street. I got to ride on a real old Western stagecoach! I have also written a poem about my friend Bill that tells of my meeting him and his accomplishments during our knowing each other. I'm including photos of me on the stagecoach and part of the cattle drive below.

THERE'S JUST SOMETHING ABOUT MONTANA
By Joyce Jackson
April 2005

THERE'S JUST SOMETHING ABOUT MONTANA
THAT MAKES YUOU WANT TO GO BACK, AGAIN AND AGAIN
IT'S HARD TO EXPLAIN, BUT ONCE YOU'VE SEEN HER
YOU FEEL JUST LIKE MONTANA'S YOUR FRIEND

IT'S MORE THAN THE MAGIC OF HER MOUNTAINS
OR THE BRILLIANCE OF HER SUNSETS, ALL AGLOW
MONTANA'S MORE THAN THE BIG SKY ABOVE YOU
OR THE FEELING THAT FILLS YOU FROM HEAD TO TOE

MONTANA'S ALL THE THINGS ABOVE AND THEN SOME
HER WARMTH MAKES YOU FEEL THAT YOU SURELY BELONG
AND IT'S HER PEOPLE AND THEIR FRIENDLY HELLO'S
THAT YOU MISS SO MUCH, WHEN YOU'RE GONE

YES, THERE'S JUST SOMETHING ABOUT MONTANA
AND I WANT TO SEE HER AGAIN, AND I WILL
TO TAKE IN THE BEAUTY OF HER MOUNTAINS
AND THE SUNSETS, THAT ARE PEACEFUL AND STILL

THE MAN FROM MONTANA
By Joyce Jackson
June 28, 2006

I met this man in nineteen seventy five
Now that seems like such a long time ago.
Mama Mae Axton brought him to Nashville
My goodness how the years have flown

He's a talented man, known through his art
A talent that was given by God above
He has never failed to give God the credit
For showering him with so much of His love

You'll see a cross with a circle around it
On every sculpture or painting that he's done
That's to show others what he already knows
That he was chosen by God as a favorite son

He's done sculptures of wildlife that roam the West
And his paintings have many stories to tell
His dream was to sculpt country music legends
And he's done some and has done them so well

He began with a sculpture only 30 inches high
Of the country legend Gentleman Jim Reeves
Then they graduated to ones bigger than life
As he wanted them remembered, don't you see?

There was Hank Williams and Ernest Tubb
Johnny Cash and Canada's Hank Snow
Buck Owens and the Possum George Jones
And, of course, Minnie Pearl you all know

He did Merle Haggard with his good looks
And Willie Nelson, with his braids and all
Yes, he even did one of the famous Garth Brooks
That's the last one he did now, as I recall

Oh, everyone loved him and the work that he did
And all wanted to be a part of his dream
But when it came time for him to be paid
Seems they all thought he should do it for free

This dream has cost him much more than most know
Like homes and business and even friends
But you can't keep him down, he hasn't lost hope
He knows he'll be the one that wins in the end

We've shared many things over these past years
Much laughter, fun times and yes, even some tears
This man from Montana has a name and a face
Bill Rains, you've made a mark no one can erase

Bill and I have been friends now for nearly 35 years and you won't run into a nicer fellow. Mae Axton brought him to Nashville and introduced him to Mary Reeves, widow of the great international country music legend, Jim Reeves. I was honored and privileged to have been Jim's personal secretary for six-and-one-half years until his untimely death. While Bill and I were talking about what he has done and how he has followed his dream, even at a personal loss, as it has cost him a great deal of money, heartache, time and expense. Still, he would not have traded this for anything and as I told him . . . "You have made a mark that no one can erase." I liked that so well that I decided I would write the poem about this man who has followed his dream, and again I am honored and privileged to have followed it with him over the years. You will be the winner Bill, when it's all said and done.

Joyce and Bill with IFCO's Johnson sisters.

Lana Nelson with award designed by Bill.

Denny Eubank, Joyce, Lana and Perla Harkins, Joyce's friend.

Rains' bronze statue of ballplayer Dave McNally.

Bill dines with Joyce and his wife Melissa.

PATSY CLINE & CHARLIE DICK ...

I am going to incorporate Patsy Cline's story, along with Charlie's, because as most of you know by now, Charlie was her husband, and he is also my friend and has been now for about 50 years. I know there are many other places in this book where I have mentioned Charlie, but he was such a great part of my life, while I lived in Nashville, and he still is, and we have so many of the same friends, that it just has to be that way, and I love it and him.

It was in 1958, that I first met Charlie, when he, Patsy and Betty Jacobs (BZ) came to Nashville to visit. They were living in Virginia at that time. They came in Linebaugh's, where a group of us were, and somehow we all agreed to go bowling. I know that Teddy, Lester and Leslie Wilburn were among the group and Charlie said that he had never bowled ten-pins before, so we all went bowling! We bowled almost all night long and just had a wonderful time. I also feel that I got to know Patsy pretty well that night. I had met her on another occasion in Louisville, but felt I really got to know her on our all-night bowling venture.

Patsy got killed in the plane crash that also claimed the lives of Cowboy Copas, Hawkshaw Hawkins and Randy Hughes, who was the pilot and Patsy's manager, on March 5, 1963. There was a time after that terrible accident that Billy Graves, Charlie and I were like The Three Musketeers. Billy was a good friend of both Charlie and Patsy, and had been a regular on *The Jimmy Dean Show,* along with Dick Flood, known as The Country Lads. Patsy was also part of Dean's show before her move to Nashville. Billy was one of the first persons that I met when I came to Nashville. In fact, I met him the first night I was in town and we became very good friends from the beginning. The three of us went places and did so many things together. I cherish all those wonderful times spent with you.

Charlie drank a great deal back then and began having quite a few parties at his house. His parties would be filled with artists and musicians and they were always a

lot of fun. There'd be folks like Dottie and Bill West, Roger Miller, Justin Tubb, Jimmy Day, and at one time or another, about every picker in Nashville would show up at Charlie's. I remember one night we were having a party there and when it got to be about five o'clock in the morning, Charlie said, "Who wants to go to Bristol, Tenn., to the races with me?" Everyone gave an excuse why they couldn't go, so I told him I would go. About an hour later, we were on the road heading to Bristol to see the races. Back then we would always go to the local races in Nashville, but this was to be my first big race and I was excited to go. We got started and got about as far as Lebanon, Tenn., when Charlie asked me if I would like to drive for awhile. He had a nice Cadillac and I told him I would, mainly because he really wasn't in any shape to drive! Charlie got in the back seat and slept almost all the way to Bristol and back then there was no Interstate. I know God was with me because I drove that 300 miles in six hours and on two-lane roads that were very crooked. We were almost to Bristol when Charlie woke up and he couldn't believe we were almost there. He had some friends there that had a motel and we checked in. By the way, we slept in separate beds! Charlie will back me up on that fact! It doesn't really matter if anyone believes that or not, because we know, right Charlie?

The race was taking place the next day after our arrival. Charlie had great seats and just when we put our feet on the first step of the grandstand, you have never seen such a down-pour! We turned around and ran back to the car. There wasn't a dry thread on either of us. We were totally drenched. The only clothes we had that were clean were our bathing suits, as we had planned to go back home immediately after the races. When we got back to the car, we changed into our bathing suits in the car with each one of us watching for the other one, in case somebody was coming. It was just too funny!

Charlie started driving back, but what he forgot about was that the racetrack was built so that when it rained, you only had to wait a short time and the track would be dry again. So we listened to the race on the way home on the radio. That was the first of many races that I went to that I never got to see, because of being rained out. This was the summer of 1963.

Charlie and I have shared so much and go back so many years that it is a little hard to write what would interest readers, but for me they have all been wonderful memories that can't be taken away nor can they be bought. They are mine and I treasure each one, but since this book is about sharing my memories, I suppose I should do just that. We shared many wonderful and fun evenings with Dottie and Bill West playing Canasta and just having a good time talking and visiting. It was good for Charlie to have friends around him that cared about him and we did care. We also shared a lot of time with just him and me. Those were fun times, too, but now that I live in Colorado, those times are few and far between.

When Joy was only two weeks old, my Mom was visiting and one day Charlie just popped in and said he was taking us to lunch. It was Joy's first outing. We went to a place called The Lazy Susan in Madison. It's no longer there, but we had a good lunch. Then Charlie told us that Maxine Brown, of the famed trio The Browns, was in the hospital. Babies weren't allowed then and Mom stayed in the car with Joy, but Charlie said he was going to get them in, and he just carried Joy in and showed her to all the nurses on the way to Maxine's room. He laid her on the foot of the bed where she slept the entire time and when we started to leave, I told him that he carried her in and he was going to carry her out! He did and joked with all the nurses again on his way out.

I remember one day back in the early 1970's when Charlie had his first little cabin cruiser. Margie Perkins, Betty (BZ) Jacobs, Charlie and me all went for a ride on Old Hickory Lake. I had no idea where Charlie was taking us, but we ended up at Hubert Long's house. Hubert, as many may remember, was one of the founders of the CMA and played such a vital part in the industry, until he had to be operated on. He had a brain tumor and the doctors removed his memory bank, so he didn't know who any of us really were, but BZ was a little familiar to him as she had the biggest boobs of anyone that I have ever known, including Dolly Parton! I remember being out on that boat one other time . . . but we won't go into that . . .It was, however, a fun afternoon.

For many years after Patsy died, Charlie, as I have said before, did his fair share of consuming the "spirits" and whenever he did this, he would get telephone happy! He would call everyone he knew and he didn't care what hour of the morning it was! Many times he would call me at two, three, four and even five in the morning, and most of the time he would end up coming over to my house, get on my telephone, and call others and get them up. Many of the calls were long distance. In fact, most of them were.

I believe it was in 1984, when I was lucky enough to acquire some tickets to the Indianapolis 500. Knowing Charlie loved the races the way he did, I asked if he would like to go with me. Of course, he wanted to and we went. We had pretty good seats near the fourth turn that heads toward the front straight-a-way. My tickets came from a friend who worked for the A.B. Dick Company. I have always thought it funny that Charlie Dick got to sit with the A.B. Dick Company section! Gordon Johncock was the winner that year. We had such a good time and it's a fun memory to recall from time-to- time.

I had Charlie and Tommy Hill over for Thanksgiving dinner 1981, and Charlie has been having Thanksgiving with my family about every year since then. He also joins us for Christmas Eve dinner and when Ruby Wright had Christmas breakfast, he joined us for that, as well, and Glenda usually has a 4th of July gathering and he joins us for that also. We feel that he is just part of our family.

Charlie used to have a New Year's Eve party at his house and they were always a lot of fun, but when he stopped drinking, he pretty much stopped having them. People didn't think they were as much fun sober as they were when they were drinking. I disagree, however, as I have always had fun with Charlie, whether it be watching the car races on his big screen TV, going to the races (that got rained out), going on little trips like the time when we went to Mobile, Ala., to celebrate Boots Barnes' 30th year in radio, sharing good friends such as Annie and Norm Armstrong from Canada, or just sitting and talking.

One of the funniest times spent with Charlie was when he and Bill Carlisle picked up me and my sisters, Glenda and Marsha, to go to the funeral home for visitation for Dottie West. Dottie was such a fun person that I told Charlie that she would love it that we were having such a great time together. Bill and Charlie together are hilarious. They

Patsy Cline in performance above. That's her husband Charlie on the right. Their story was depicted in the 1985 box office hit 'Sweet Dreams,' which had Jessica Lange as Patsy and Ed Harris as Charlie.

would not let us be sad and that was a good thing. I could almost hear Dottie saying, "Way to Go, Charlie." I wish everyone could have had the opportunity to spend just one evening with Charlie Dick and Bill Carlisle. They kept us in stitches and I'm so thankful I have this great memory to share. I'm so blessed because I have had many of these wonderful opportunities.

Charlie, you know how special you are and have always been to me. You're my friend, my brother, my confidant and I love you now and for always. We've had such memorable times together in the past and I know that we will continue to share many more fun-filled years, but let's leave the fish bowl filled with flowers, OK? You're one in a million GTC and I love you.

*Charlie, Joyce and Norm Armstrong,
a Canadian friend.*

Patsy's face depicted on a decorator magnet.

*Charlie, Anne Armstrong,
Joyce and Norm Armstrong.*

Charlie and David McCormick.

Charlie with friends (from left) Barbara and Ray Baker and Leo Jackson.

Charlie relaxing with showbiz buddies Bill Carlisle and Stu Basore.

Charlie with Joyce's mom, Sue Gray.   *Charlie and Joyce.*

Prankster Charlie puckers up for pal Leo Jackson.

ARTISTS that I have met, but really didn't know very well;

however, we have shared a memory or two, so I wanted to put them in this book:

ROY CLARK - Roy was a friend of Dean Manuel's and Dean brought him by the office several times. I also knew his wife Barbara.

PEE WEE KING - Pee Wee used to come by our hospitality suite during the DJ Conventions and once I ran into him at K-Mart on Gallatin Road and we had a nice visit.

WADE RAY - Wade was manager of the Gibson Guitar office in Nashville for a while and we got to be pretty good friends when I had my office close by at RCA.

CHARLIE WALKER - I have known Charlie for years, as he and Jim were friends, and I first met him at Jim's house, but we never ran in the same circles.

NAT STUCKEY - Met Nat right after he and his wife Ann come to Nashville, but knew Ann better than Nat. Nat cut one of our publishing company's songs, which Vic McAlpin wrote, titled "Plastic Saddle." Good song!

GEORGE STRAIT - Only met George one time when I worked for Frank and Jeanie Oakley. We had a Willie Nelson gift shop on 16th Avenue and George had a gift shop right next door, and one day he came in and I went over to his shop and met him. He is a really good-looking man. Looks better in person than on TV!

T. GRAHAM BROWN - The only time that I met T. Graham was in Alabama at a George Jones concert, and it was George's birthday. Mae Axton, Tammy Wells and me all went down for the celebration.

HANK SNOW - Hank only lived three or four blocks from me in Madison, and I used to go by his house and take him songs and, of course, have seen him many times at the Opry and during various music industry events.

CONNIE SMITH - I met Connie right after she came to Nashville, but never really got to know her well. Have been to her recording sessions and love her particular style of singing. There is no one that can sing "How Great Thou Art" quite like Connie.

MARTY STUART - I have met Marty on several different occasions, but do not know him really. I saw and chatted with both he and Connie (they're married) at the Music Valley area Cracker Barrel several years ago. That's the last time I've seen either of them.

Joyce and Ray Price

RAY PRICE - I love Ray's vocals and while he lived in Nashville, we would run into each other occasionally, but I didn't know him well. My brother-in-law Stu worked the road with Ray at one time in his band. I have many favorite Ray Price songs, but I love "For The Good Times" written by Kris Kristofferson, "Are You Sure" and "Night Life" written by Willie Nelson.

WAYNE NEWTON - Met Wayne in the RCA Building. He was visiting Chet Atkins and Chet introduced him to me. His recording of "Daddy, Don't You Walk So Fast" was just out and already showing signs of becoming the hit it eventually was.

JERRY LEE LEWIS - Ralph Emery used to do an early TV show and I went there many times, once when Jerry Lee was his guest artist and Ralph introduced us, but I do not really know him.

CAL SMITH - Dean Manuel and Cal were good friends and right after Cal came to Nashville to join E.T.'s Texas Troubadours, Dean brought him by Jim Reeves Enterprises. I was around Cal many times after that and became friends with Darlene, his wife. I believe that Cal is now doing shows in Branson, Mo. I'm sure many will recall his big hit "Country Bumpkin," I, for one, love that song and love you Cal, and Darlene.

KENNY ROGERS - The only time that I met Kenny was at the hospital when he came to see Dottie West after the accident that took her life. Dottie's children and I were all in the hospital waiting room when Kenny came in. He visited briefly with all of us until they let him see Dottie. Dottie died not long after that visit. It was kind of Kenny to come see Dottie and even though it was not a happy time for us, I am glad that I can at least share the memory of his kindness.

Minnie Pearl with Joy.

MINNIE PEARL - Minnie was one of the funniest women I have ever known, not only on stage, but behind-the-scenes, as well. We used to have some fun conversations in the little dressing room-restroom backstage at the Ryman. It was in this same room where I first met June Carter Cash and her sisters Anita and Helen. They have all since passed on, but oh, the talks that went on in that little room! When Mary Reeves formed her softball team The Reev-Ettes, Minnie was one of our team members, as was Dottie West and Kitty Wells. I'd go out to Minnie's house and give her the shirt she was to wear with our team name on it. What a lady, and I'm so blessed to have known her, brief as it was. Thanks for all the laughs, Minnie. (Minnie died March 4, 1996.)

ROY ACUFF - Roy is the undisputed "King" of country music. At the Opry, he had the number one dressing room and on the door was a message that read something like "Nothing's going to happen today, that me and the Good Lord can't fix." That might not be the exact wording, but it's close. I didn't know Mr. Roy personally, but he surely had my respect and I met and talked with him on several occasions. He died Nov. 23, 1992.

MICKEY NEWBURY - Mickey was such a tremendous talent and was one of the ones who had a houseboat and tied up with us, as I tell in the Hank Cochran story. We did have some fun on those

Jean Shepard, Roy Acuff, Glenda and Joyce.

boats and I loved Mickey's rendition of "The American Trilogy" which he put together and was such a big hit for Elvis. I was so sorry to learn of his death on Sept. 28, 2002.

LORRIE MORGAN - Although I have seen Lorrie perform on the Opry many times, I only met her once when she was on WSM's *Waking Crew* radio show broadcast live at The Opryland Hotel. Stu was a part of that show, playing steel guitar, and he's the one who introduced me to Lorrie. Our paths crossed, so I wanted to mention her. She is a wonderful talent and I'm glad for her success. Love her song "What Part Of No (Don't You Understand)." We've all used that line often since that song came out.

GEORGE MORGAN - George is Lorrie's dad, and was a great singer. I got to meet him one time, when Clarence Reynolds, Commerce Union Bank executive, introduced us. I had an appointment with Clarence and while waiting to see him, George was in with Clarence, and the banker asked me to come in, as he thought I knew George. When I told him that I had never met him before, Clarence said it was about time I did. I agreed, as did George. I so respected his talent, with hits like "Candy Kisses," "Room

Full Of Roses" and the Vic McAlpin-penned hit "Almost." (George Morgan died July 7, 1975, and was posthumously inducted into the Country Music Hall of Fame in 1998.)

DALLAS FRAZIER - Dallas, you are one in a million! What a writer! I don't even remember when we first met. Guess that really doesn't matter. What does matter is that we have been friends for a very long time. That is something that I will always treasure. One thing that I remember about you, Dallas, is when you would go visit your Mom, you would always bring back some smoked salmon to share with some of us. Was that ever good! You and Ray Baker made quite a writer and publisher team a few years back. Ray wrote a song that Jim Reeves cut, titled "There's A Heartache Following Me." Ray and I worked together at Jim Reeves Enterprises. Dallas began writing at an early age and had a big hit with "Alley Oop" by The Hollywood Argyles, and then there was Jack Greene's career hit "There Goes My Everything," and who could or would want to forget "Elvira" by The Oak Ridge Boys. I'm so happy and proud to call you friend. I saw and talked with Dallas and Ray, along with their wives Sharon and Barbara, at the funeral home, during the services for Leo Jackson in May 2008.

Joyce, Boxcar and Charlean Keller.

BOXCAR WILLIE - I only met Boxcar a few times. He had a train museum in the Music Valley area right next to the Wax Museum, and one time when some of my Montana friends were in town visiting, we went by Boxcar's museum and he happened to be in, so Charlean Keller and I had our picture made with him. I really can't say I knew him well, but at least we did meet.

FELICE & BOUDLEAUX BRYANT - I knew Felice much better than Boudleaux, as she used to come by and visit with me when we had Jim Reeves Enterprises in the Primrose Center in Madison, and many times she and I would walk over to Patterson's Restaurant and either have a bite to eat or just have a cup of coffee. She was always so full of energy. I just loved her. Boudleaux was quiet and a laid-back kind of person, but what a team of writers they were, with songs like "Bye, Bye, Love" and "Wake Up, Little Susie" cut by the Everly Brothers, "Blue Boy" by Jim Reeves, and an official Tennessee state song, "Rocky Top." Boudleaux passed away in 1987 and Felice died on April 22, 2003. Jointly they were inducted into the Songwriters Hall of Fame in 1972, and the Country Music Hall of Fame in 1991.

JOHNNY CARVER - Johnny used to be one of our Open Road Music Publishing Company writers and basically just as a co-worker who I didn't see too often, that was how we knew one another. He's really a nice man and very talented, and he had the big hit "Tie A Yellow Ribbon ('Round The Old Oak Tree)." Johnny had the country version and Tony Orlando & Dawn the pop hit on the same song. Personally, I liked your version better, Johnny. Glad I knew you.

DICKEY LEE - I used to see Dickey a lot during the time that I was in the RCA Building and we became pretty good friends. I haven't heard much about him lately, but I do know that he lost his wife in 2008. I loved his hit "9,999,999 Tears." What a clever song (written by Razzy Bailey). I also loved his version of "Never Ending Song Of Love." Among Dickey's own #1 writing achievements: "She Thinks I Still Care" and "Let's Fall To Pieces Together." I miss seeing and visiting with you, Dickey. Thanks for some fun times and good memories.

REBA McENTIRE - The one time I met Reba was when Mae Axton was toasted in February 1988. Proceeds from that toast went to the Spina Bifida Association of America. It was held at the Nashville Vanderbilt Plaza Hotel on West End, and many were in attendance that night, including Willie Nelson. These two have been helped in their careers by Mae. I had been invited by the Hands Across The Table charity, of which I had been a part, and they were contributors to this particular charity. Reba and I actually met when we were in the restroom! We chatted for a little while and she was very excited, as I believe she was about to be married to Narvel Blackstock, or maybe had just been asked to marry him. I know she was one happy person and I'm glad I got to share that little part of her life with her, and now with you. Thanks Reba, our paths only crossed for those brief moments in the restroom, but I'm glad they did. I love her recordings of "You're The First Time I've Thought About Leaving" and "Somebody Should Leave." Those are just a couple of my favorites, but she's had hit after hit in her career, and I also loved her in her self-titled TV show. (Still see its reruns occasionally.)

GEORGE JONES - I have mentioned George in the Wilburn Brothers' section and there isn't too much else to write about him, except to say that I first met him not long after Jean Shepard moved to Bell Grimes Lane. I was there visiting with Jean when George and George Riddle came by. I don't remember exactly when that was, but was probably late 1959 or early 1960. Anyway, it was before Jean and Hawkshaw Hawkins were married and before George moved to Tennessee. He used to come into Linebaugh's quite a bit back then and would join us. He always had a tall tale to tell. I never did know if they were for real, but we listened, and now they are part of my memory of George Jones, and I'd listen to more of them if given a chance. George has had so many hits, and I like all of them 'cause I'm a George Jones Fan! But I do have some favorites like "Walk Through This World With Me," "Four-O-Thirty-Three" and "He Stopped Loving Her Today." Thanks *Possum* for the memories, especially the musical ones. I would not take anything for the pleasure of having met you. George was inducted into the Country Music Hall of Fame in 1992.

LITTLE JIMMY DICKENS - About the only time that I have been around "Tater" (his show business nickname, due to his debut hit "Take An Old Cold 'Tater And Wait") was backstage at the Opry. I always loved talking with him, as he reminded me of a bantam rooster. He's only 4-feet, 11-inches tall and seemed to be everywhere at once. What a great little performer. The last time I saw him perform was in Carthage, Texas, in 2006. He was part of the show featuring Mac Davis and Johnny Lee for the Texas

Joyce and Jimmy.

Country Music Hall of Fame inductee night. Even though now in his 80's, Jimmie's still a fine performer. I would not think of leaving you out of my book 'Tater, because you are rare and very special. Thanks for crossing my path! "May The Bird Of Paradise Fly Up Your Nose". . . just had to add that popular song title of yours.

CLAUDE GRAY - Claude used to drop by Jim Reeves Enterprises quite often, as he and Jim were friends and fellow Texans. Claude has also enjoyed some hit records since we met, and I just wanted to include him. His recording of "Family Bible" (written by Willie Nelson) is awesome and "I'll Just Have A Cup Of Coffee (Then I'll Go)" is also memorable.

SONNY JAMES - I know Sonny because of his many recordings and seeing him at various music business happenings, but he was always so nice. He's a very quiet-spoken person and seems to love people. I've talked with him on many occasions, but that's about it; however, I love his recordings of "Young Love" and "That's Me Without You." Called *The Southern Gentleman,* the name fits him perfectly. I found him to be truly a gentle man.

LORENE MANN - Lorene and I have been friends for many years, along with another wonderful lady, Marie Wilson. Lorene was never a big star, but some will remember that she's the writer of Rex Allen's hit recording "Don't Go Near The Indians." She also recorded duets with Archie Campbell and Justin Tubb, and she and I wrote a song together, which has never been recorded called "I Can't Help But Let You Tell Me A Lie." I still think it's a pretty good song. Wish someone would record it, don't you, Lorene. Thanks for many years of knowing you and for some memorable times together.

BUDDY HARMAN - I knew Buddy many years and he was part of what the music industry considered an "A" Team of session musicians. I suppose that Buddy has been the drummer for just about everybody who has ever recorded in Nashville. He was a staff drummer on the Opry and Buddy was also an avid bowler and part of our Music Business Mixed League. We bowled on that league for several years. Buddy died Aug. 21, 2008, causing Nashville to lose another great musician. He'll be missed.

BUFORD PUSSER.- I met Buford when my office was still at RCA, and he was in town to record. He was also slated to give a few speeches about his life and the movie that depicted his life. Many will remember that Joe

Joyce and Buddy Harman.

Don Baker was Buford in the box office hit "Walking Tall." As Sheriff, Buford tried hard to clean up the corruption in and around his west Tennessee county. RCA had a reception for him while he was in town, and I was invited. He visited with all of us as much as he could and told many stories about how these corrupt people had killed his wife and threatened him many times. He carried scars where they had beat him

Crime fighter Buford Pusser (that's Joyce on his left) with the gals at RCA Records.

on many occasions. He was so interesting, but was killed not too long after that time frame, on his way home one night. He had a car accident that was suspect, with many feeling the car had been tampered with, causing the wreck. I don't know, but I'm glad I had the opportunity to meet and visit with the real Buford Pusser and I personally feel Joe Don did the best version of Buford (as there were sequels). Meeting Buford made a wonderful memory for me.

JAN HOWARD - Jan Howard is another artist that I have known since she moved to Nashville, while still married to Harlan Howard, the Hall of Fame songwriter. We were both involved with some events and charities that took place in Billings. Although I have known Jan some 50 years, we have never really done things together as I have with so many others. However, I have always cared so much for Jan and feel she was and is a tremendous asset to the industry. She was the girl singer on Bill Anderson's TV show and made hit duets with him, including the #1 "For Loving You."

JOHN CONLEE - I met John before he came out with his self-penned 1978 breakthrough hit "Rose Colored Glasses." He was a friend to Bud Logan, of The Blue Boys, and a recording artist for our Shannon Records label. Bud was John's producer and he used to come by our office quite frequently. He was also a Kentucky boy, so I did get to know him pretty good. We also attended some of the same music-related functions. John's a very down-to-earth kind of guy with a "what you see is what you get" sort of attitude. I've always liked that about you, John, and appreciate your staying true to yourself. Glad to add you to the list of those who crossed my path on the music scene.

Joyce and Charlie McCoy.

CHARLIE McCOY - Charlie is someone I always enjoyed being around. He's never called me anything but "J.J." - and we used to bowl on the same league. Charlie was league president, and we always bowled Sunday nights. Called The Music Business Mixed League, it had artists, secretaries, managers and promoters, all of whom were part of our music industry as members. In my opinion, no one plays harmonica like Charlie McCoy. He is definitely a stylist. We used to have get-togethers at Charlie's house where we'd play volleyball, went swimming and all-in-all just had a wonderful time. Thanks for all the good memories, Charlie.

TOMMY CASH - Tommy is another artist who comes to mind. Although we saw one another many times over the years, we really didn't do things together. Tommy's the younger brother of Johnny Cash, and a recording artist in his own right, with a few hit singles, such as "Six White Horses" and "Rise and Shine." The one and only time we did do something together was when my daughter Joy was about 4 months old. My high school was having a reunion and I wanted to go, and Tommy was at Jim Reeves Enterprises for some reason and I mentioned the reunion. He said I could ride up with him, as he was playing a date near Louisville, so I rode with him. Tommy dropped me off at the airport, where my girlfriend, Perla Harkins, picked me up. It was a nice three-hour ride and I got to know him better than I had before. Thanks for the ride, Tommy, and for another good memory to share.

JOHNNY PAYCHECK - In 1958, when I was introduced to Johnny, he was then called Donny Young. He came to town with Darrell McCall, and I believe they were friends from Ohio, the best I remember. Johnny Paycheck is now best known for his recording "Take This Job And Shove It." Even though Johnny was considered an outlaw and a kinda rebel, he was always very nice to me and I am glad we met all those many years ago. (Johnny died Feb. 18, 2003.)

TOM T. HALL - Tom T. Hall is one of Nashville's more prolific songwriters and also a hit-making artist. Too many years have passed since we first met, for me to remember just when or where it was - but it must have been in 1964 or 1965. It was way before he and Miss Dixie got married. After we moved our offices to Madison Street in 1967, he used to come by quite frequently. I heard Jeannie C. Riley's smash hit song "Harper Valley PTA" long before she recorded it. Of course, Tom T. is the writer of this classic! He later started recording himself and had many hits. One of my very favorites, and evidently a favorite of a lot of folks, is "(Old Dogs-Children and) Watermelon Wine." I was invited to his and Dixie's house for a Halloween party once and it was so much fun! We did attend many of the same music-oriented affairs over the years, so I was able to visit some with both Tom T. and Dixie during those times. Love your writing, Tom T., and wish I had gotten to know you better. You're a classic yourself.

EDDIE RABBITT - Eddie Rabbitt and fellow songwriter Even Stevens ran around together. Whenever you'd see one, most likely you'd see the other. They used to drop by my office at RCA and I always loved for them to come in and visit, because they were super great guys. I loved their stories, but was never quite sure if they were for real or not. Both were extremely talented and were well-known co-writers. One of Eddie's most-famous songs he wrote was "Kentucky Rain," which Elvis Presley recorded. With Even, he also co-wrote "Drinkin' My Baby (Off My Mind)" and "Suspicions," among others. But one of my favorite Eddie Rabbitt recordings was their co-write "I Love A Rainy Night" (with David Malloy). Thanks for coming by my office to visit! (Eddie passed away, at age 56, from cancer on May 7, 1998.)

MEL McDANIELS - Mel McDaniels and songwriter Royce Porter also came by my RCA office one day around 1972 or 1973. I knew Royce, as he was one of our publishing company writers, so he brought Mel by to introduce him. Mel had just came in from Alaska. The last time I saw Mel was in 2004, when he came into the Discount Tobacco Outlet, where I was working at the time, and bought cigarettes. Mel is not well now, but the Opry star has enjoyed several hit recordings, and one of his biggest and my favorite, is "Baby's Got Her Blue Jeans On." Thanks Royce for introducing us.

WEBB PIERCE - Webb Pierce was a major star, and our paths crossed many times after I moved to Nashville. He enjoyed numerous hit recordings in his career, such as "I Don't Care," "There Stands The Glass" and one that I always liked best by him, "Slowly." I found out later that this one was written by Tommy Hill, who worked in Jim's band at one time and was a good friend of mine. I saw and got to know Webb a little bit, when he attended the ROPE get-togethers. Webb's guitar-shaped swimming pool proved a big draw among tourists in town. Tour buses would go to his home, then situated across the street from Ray Stevens, on Curtiswood Circle, known as *Millionaire's Circle* because on that circle was the Governor's mansion, Minnie Pearl's home, Ronnie Milsap's, Webb's, and Ray's. The buses irked Stevens, who made much ado about their invasion of his privacy. I have always respected the fact that Webb sure seemed to know how to pick his material. (Webb died Feb. 24, 1991, and was belatedly inducted into the Country Music Hall of Fame in 2000.)

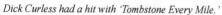

Dick Curless had a hit with 'Tombstone Every Mile.'   *Country Hall of Famer Floyd Tillman & Joyce.*

ARTISTS THAT I WISH I COULD HAVE MET . . .

Although I was in the music business for nearly half a century, there are many artists that I did not meet, but have come to admire so much, I sincerely wish that I could have had an opportunity to have at least met the following talents, great artists all:

Billy (Crash) Craddock - "Rub It In"

John Schneider - "I've Been Around Enough To Know"

Ricky Van Shelton - "I'll Leave This World Loving You"

Alan Jackson - "Here In the Real World" I met Roger, his guitar player, who would come in to Discount Tobacco Outlet when I worked there.

Gene Autry - Loved his radio show *The Melody Ranch* as a youngster.

Hank Williams, Sr. - When he passed from the scene on Jan. 1, 1953, a Louisville radio station had a *Hank Williams Day* and I skipped school to listen to all the records they played that day.

Elton Britt - I loved to hear him yodel (remember his "Chime Bells"?).

Bob Wills - Cindy Walker told me all about him and what a great guy The King of Western Swing was. Of course, he recorded numerous Cindy Walker songs, including "You're From Texas."

Clint Black - He got a chance to record with King of the Cowboys, Roy Rogers!

Don Williams - "Lord, I Hope This Day Is Good."

Garth Brooks - "Friends in Low Places."

Bing Crosby - The first film star to record a Cindy Walker song, and make it a hit!

Charlie Daniels - "The Devil Went Down to Georgia."

John Denver - Got to see him perform live once, when I was visiting England.

Donna Fargo - "The Happiest Girl in The Whole USA."

Tennessee Ernie Ford - He could sing country, pop or gospel equally well.

Vince Gill - Saw him perform a couple of times, but never met him. I hope to meet him one of these days, so I can personally thank him for his kind words about Jim Reeves.

Wilma Lee Cooper and Joyce at the Opry.

Joyce links up to 'Gone' hitmaker Ferlin Husky.

JOYCE'S SCRAPBOOK

Flanking Joyce at the 2009 SOURCE Awards are Dan and Perla Harkins, and Sherry Lange and Neil Williamson (Sheriff, Springfield, Ill.).

Jim Reeves, an RCA publicity shot.

Jim just doing his thing, singin' his song..

Jim

Jim with his pet Cheyenne.

Jim

Joyce's sister Glenda with Jim.

Hawkshaw Hawkins autographed his photo for the author.

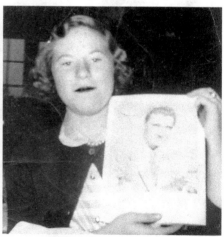

Ernest Tubb with co-stars Doyle & Teddy.   *Joyce with autographed picture of Carl Smith.*

Texas Troubadour Ernest Tubb.

Joyce with Porter Wagoner backstage.

Smilin' Eddie Hill, a DJ, and Joyce.

Fiddler Gordon Terry and Jan, Joyce's sis.

Joyce and singer Don Gibson.

Joyce with a treasured Wilburn Brothers LP.

*Square dance king Ben Smathers greets
Norma Jean and Joyce after the show.*

Mae offers birthday gal Joyce a card.

Joyce's friend Coleen Johnson Ruperto.

Top steel guitarist Stu Basore.

Jim Reeves fan Beckie Mawa of Zimbabwe.

*Joyce in England with Tony Wall, Steve Moorewood and
David Bussey during her guest spot with DJ Tex Milne..*

Carl Butler poses with Joyce.

Leo, Joyce, Bill Walker and Florence Keels during Christmas 1964 at Mary's house.

Sister act: Marsha, Glenda, Joyce, Jean, her sis Frances, and Jan during Christmas 1958.

Norwegian artist Arne Benoni and Leo.

The Wilburn Brothers band.

Coleen Johnson Ruperto in her calico outfit in 1965.

Famed DJ T. Tommy Cutrer and pianist Jim Pierce.

Joyce, Leo and Lani, Jim Reeves' niece.

*Mogens and Hanne Jensen, of Denmark, with ex-Blue Boy
James Kirkland and Lani Arnold, Jim Reeves' niece.*

*Joyce, Tony Wall & David Bussey,
Jim's Fan Club leader for 25 years.*

Neil Williamson and Fast Eddy Ruebling, DJ, WQNA-Springfield, Ill.

Joyce with Jim Reeves' nieces (from left) Kay, Lani and Carolyn at Country Hall of Fame, 1999.

More Mementos . . .

To Joyce

Dear,

Ruby

Friend's
Credit Card
This Card is not for material
things but is to give you
credit for being the greatest
in the world and for that
You Deserve Credit

Joyce —
Once in a while...

Someone comes along
and in that one
you see
love and friendship
wrapped in one
that's what you mean
to me.
You gave me so
much
a touch, a
smile ...
someone like
you
comes along
just once
in a
while.
I love you!
Mae

From Ruby Wright Taylor, above; & Mae Boren Axton, right.

MEET THE AUTHOR

Joy and Mom

JOYCE GRAY JACKSON is a native of Simpson County, Ky., who grew up in the Pewee Valley community near Louisville, one of four daughters and a son born to Sue and Wiley Gray. While growing up, she enjoyed going to the movies to see singing cowboy heroes like Roy Rogers and Tex Ritter, while also tuning in to the sounds of country music, notably recordings by favorites Eddy Arnold, Hank Williams, Kitty Wells, Jean Shepard, The Wilburn Brothers and Jim Reeves. Little did she dream that one day she would meet most of her musical heroes, and even work several years side by side with the renowned *Gentleman Jim* Reeves.

Only 10 days after arriving in *Music City USA,* Joyce was hired as personal secretary at Jim Reeves Enterprises, which encompassed such subsidiary companies as music publishing firms like Acclaim, and later an independent label, Shannon Records, producing successes such as "Wake Me Into Love" by Bud Logan and Wilma Burgess.

In addition to having co-written songs herself, Joyce has inspired two successful compositions: Justin Tubb's "Take a Letter, Miss Gray," a 1963 Top 10, and Merle Kilgore's tribute to PeWee Valley, recorded by pop music stalwart Vaughn Monroe. Besides working with Shannon Records, Joyce assisted Mae Axton at DPI Records. She has also worked on behalf of Dottie West, Floyd Cramer, the Ernest Tubb Record Shops and the Willie Nelson Museum and Theatre. Joyce has donated her time to such events as the annual Disc Jockey Convention, the 1989 Montana Centennial, the Hands

Across the Table charity, and has helped preserve the traditions of country music through involvement as a charter member of the Reunion Of Professional Entertainers (ROPE), a non-profit organization comprised of industry veterans.

For these many efforts, Joyce was honored as a 2009 recipient of the prestigious SOURCE Award, given annually by the non-profit SOURCE Foundation, to recognize women executives who have pioneered in all facets of the Nashville music scene.

She was wed to the late guitarist Leo Jackson, with whom she had a daughter, Joy, truly her pride and joy. Joyce is recognized as an authority on Jim Reeves' history. Today, the author resides in Colorado, mainly to be near her daughter and grandchildren. Her ties to Nashville are strong, however, and she shuttles back and forth, whenever an occasion warrants it.

The Gray clan (from left): Wiley, Sue, Jerry, Joyce, Glenda, Jan and Marsha, 1959.

Mom and Dad Sue and Wiley Gray with Jerry, 4, and Joyce, 2.

Joyce and Mae Axton at Joy's wedding to former hubby Dennis Shull.

Joyce Jackson in 1959.

CPSIA information can be obtained
at www.ICGtesting.com
Printed in the USA
BVHW091754060222
628185BV00010B/317

9 780963 268464